What Kind Of Game Is This?.
Can Anyone Play?

Emilio Briones Iglesias

María de la Paz
Barbosa González

What Kind of Game Is This? Can Anyone Play?

JESUS BRIONES

Fulton Books
Meadville, PA

Published by Fulton Books 2024

ISBN 979-8-88731-716-8 (paperback)
ISBN 979-8-88731-717-5 (digital)

Printed in the United States of America

Part One

Mi Camisa Es de Manta Rayada, Mis Huaraches de Tres Agujeros

It was a rainy morning in the City by the Desert. Under the brim of his old fedora, he could see in the cold, hard, wet pavement reflections prompted by the dawn's first light. A telling teardrop he could not contain! It had been a quiet night in downtown Tucson; the reflections in the pavement had a hypnotic effect. They laid naked the elusiveness of reality and struggle and futility of the human condition. As soon as Barista Del Barrio opened, he would be there to get a chorizo and beans burro, with an Horchesso Chaser to soothe his weary soul! Wait! Wait! This is not a novel about that hard-boiled, tough-as-nails, hard-luck private investigator Emilio Noir, cursed with a fly that was always open! This is about some lines I want to address to Carlos that are meant for all my kids.

But since Emilio Noir and I are close friends, I will probably digress and continue to mention him now and then.

Sooo, dear Carlos,

We hardly ever see each other, and this is my best attempt to stay in touch. I could talk about the weather or a long list of other subjects that may or may not be of interest to you.

But instead, I want to tell you about your background on my side of the family. Of course, don't worry, I will supplement the stories with my commentaries—especially about how I am continually surprised by the fragile and fleeting nature of life and what we think really matters.

Maybe this sounds like a lot of soul-searching books out there, but it's not. I think it is a way for us to create a connection. Long ago, we *outgrew*, for lack of a better word, the connection we shared when you guys were growing up. Even if we had spoken more, our versions of life would be different, at least. Sons and their fathers often see things differently, everything from the mechanics of their relationship to what matters most.

But I will be as accurate as I can. Just as the color of a grasshopper is green by virtue of what he does, what I say will be organically colored, the product of a blessed and wonderful life that began in Mexico.

Just writing you now, I feel like we are getting closer, like going outside and throwing the old baseball around. If we were Klingons, we'd call it Rustai. Then again, if we were Klingons, we wouldn't be talking about emotion or nostalgia in the first place!

Emotion is what got me started on this idea a while back. We were having dinner at a client's home—we have been blessed with the kindest clients imaginable—and they asked me about my background. As I talked, before I could check myself, I was weeping like a Magdalena. At the end of the evening (after slobber dried), my friends suggested that I write about some of the things we shared that evening so my kids may know about them.

When I told Emilio Noir (EN) I would be doing this, he told me I must be pretty far up my own ass if I want to write about my emotions. I quickly dismissed him though.

The main reason I got started with this, however, is that I have been working sometimes with the Picard. One of these times when we were talking instead of working, I told him about a dream I *recently* had. In the dream, I was getting ready to embark on a trip, a very long trip. I was not sure if I would ever see my loved ones again. There with me was something or somebody (this part gets fuzzy) helping me put things in order for the trip. This presence felt all-powerful, ready to grant me any wish in the form of gifts for each and every one of my loved ones. Each gift would represent my very best wish for each one of them.

I begin to instruct this somebody what the gifts are going to be. I don't know if everyone is there waiting or I'm working off a list of names. At this point, I think the Picard will be curious to know what I left for his father. So I explain how when Sergio's turn comes up, and I am debating what to give him, and just like with the others, I quickly discard the obvious nonvalue items, such as Swiss bank accounts and other liquid assets. In this dream, money has no value.

After a great deal of thought, I end up with a short list for Sergio: one is *for him* to "lose his interest in liquor" and stop drinking; the other is to give him the "desire to read." *I tell the Picard I decided to gift him the desire to read.*

The Picard thinks about it for a while and asks me, "So you want to give him the gift of him reading books?" I tell him no, that is not the gift. I explain that when you wish something, you have to be very clear and careful what you are wishing for. Of course, I want him to read, but more than that, and whether he reads or not, what I wish to give him is the *desire* to read. The desire would make him eager to read; what he would surely learn from that would surely cure his alcoholism.

Another reason I am writing this is that if I had to go somewhere, and I had something to give as a going-away present, I pray that I am granted a gift that I can intertwine in these lines. The gift I pray for would be like "the desire" in Sergio's gift. I pray that some morsel of wisdom finds its way here, one that would bring with it a component of some value to someone, however intangible it might appear on the surface.

I trust it's self-evident that the action of writing, for someone of my era and background, is like getting a tooth pulled. The odds are that nothing here is new, but after all these years, I continue to be amused by the subjects that occupy me here. It's like the amusement felt by the deer in the middle of the road, in the middle of the night, that suddenly gets hit by the high beams of a semitruck coming at full speed at him. The deer does not have to know what it is that is coming at him to be amused by it.

Let's start with the basics: the Briones and the Barbosas. My parents, Emilio Briones Iglesias and Maria de La Paz Barbosa de Briones, were born in Mexico at the turn of the century. They were children at the time of the Mexican Revolution, which was the first social revolution of the twentieth century (if you believe textbooks). The fighting lasted from 1910 to 1920.

The revolution started as a rebellion against the dictatorship of Porfirio Diaz and the Porfiriato, as they called the time of his rule. The intellectual Francisco I. Madero with his motto "Sufragio efectivo, no reeleccion" channeled the country's collective frustration against the dictator. The rebellion culminated with the exile of Diaz to Paris and the election of Madero as president in 1911.

Once the elections were over, however, the blood really started to flow.

As ever, special interests were thick and stuck to everything. The United States was one of several power players. The assassination of president-elect Madero together with Vice President Jose Maria Pino Suarez was accomplished with help from the US ambassador to Mexico, Henry Lane Wilson. In one of many examples of illegitimate involvement, the US allowed the troops of Jose Victoriano Huerta to cross the border at Nogales, supplied them with guns and ammunition, transportation, supplies, etc. so they could return to Mexico fully fortified through Agua Prieta and attack Pancho Villa from behind.

All the while the US government had an agreement not to interfere in return for Villa not touching US interests or US citizens in Mexico. In retaliation to this betrayal, Villa made his historic raid into Columbus, New Mexico.

Most books on the subject do not contain anything about innocent bystanders in Mexico, children like my mother and father, hapless victims swept up in the storm of violence. I have not read anything describing the despair and feelings of hopelessness that set in when people were broken into hard pieces by the bloodshed, the destruction, the loss of a mother, a brother, or the ultimate pain, a son or daughter.

When loss is that personal, you no longer care who won or lost, who fought bravely, who cowered. You don't care why. Your own loss is so enormous that you have no room for others—you suddenly find yourself hopelessly lost, alone, feeling *forever cold, forever hungry.*

You can read about the players, the ideologies, the goals, massacres such as the Decena Tragica. The bloody events took place from February 9 to 19, 1913. In the rare opportunities when I would ask my father about his parents and other family members, he would tell me how his father and mother, and I think he mentioned a brother maybe even a sister, disappeared during this Decena Trágica. They were never seen or heard from again.

FLEEING FROM THE DANGER ZONE
DURING THE "DECENA TRAGICA"

Even though there are differences of opinion on the merit of the revolution, you cannot deny the strength and dignity shown by the downtrodden in the face of extreme shortages of food and other essentials. They managed to push through drama and misfortune and build new lives. The music that came out of this tumultuous time is extraordinary. The country at the time was 90 percent indigenous, and their capacity to communicate tragedy in a way that helped to heal themselves was almost supernatural—not to be confused with "magical".

This photo of "Soldaderas" which has made it
around the world is titled "LA ADELITA"

En lo alto de la abrupta serranía
Acampado se encontraba un regimiento
Y una moza que valiente los seguía
Locamente enamorada del sargento.

Popular entre la tropa era Adelita
La mujer que el sargento idolatraba
Que además de ser valiente era bonita
Que hasta el mismo coronel la respetaba

Y se oía que decía, aquel que tanto la quería:

Y si Adelita se fuera con otro
La seguiría por tierra y por mar
Si por mar en un buque de Guerra
Si por tierra en un tren militar

Y si Adelita quisiera ser mi esposa
Y si Adelita ya fuera mi mujer
Le compraría un vestido de seda
Para llevarla a bailar al cuartel.

Y después que terminó la cruel batalla
Y la tropa regreso a su campamento
Por la voz de una mujer que sollozaba
Esta plegaria se oyó en el campamento:

Y al oírla el sargento temeroso
De perder para siempre a su adorada
Escondiendo su dolor bajo el Rebozo
A su amada le canto de esta manera:

Y se oía que decía
Aquel que tanto la quería:

Y si acaso yo muero en la Guerra
Y mi cadáver lo van a sepultar
Adelita por Dios te lo ruego
Que por mí no vayas a llorar

Such is the world that greeted my mother and father when they were born.

We know very little about my father's family. He lived with his parents, Antonio Briones and Julia Iglesias, in Mexico City. We believe he was born at the turn of the century, which means he was about ten years old during the infamous Decena Trágica. After the sudden disappearance of his parents, he drifted for a while, and eventually as a young adult, he found his way to the industrial northern city of Monterrey, Mexico, and to a job in a furniture factory. There he learned to be a carpenter.

We know more about my mother's family. She was born January 24, 1905, to Cipriano Barbosa and Josefina Gonzales. Her grandparents were Juan Barbosa and Guadalupe Fernandes. On her mother's side, her grandmother's name was Dorotea Gonzales. She was the second of at least six children: Lupe, Maria de la Paz, Juan, Cipriano, Enrique, and Josefina. We know my mother's mother died at a young age, but not the circumstances.

She was born in Northern Mexico in Ciudad Lerdo, Durango. Ciudad Lerdo was elevated to the status of village and given the name of Villa Lerdo De Tejada in 1864 by Don Benito Juarez himself.

This agricultural region is known by its cultivation of cotton, wheat, and grapes. This explains Tio Cipriano Barbosa's background in vineyards, skills he used in pioneering the cultivation of grapes in the now-thriving agricultural community of Caborca, Sonora.

Hoy mi guitarra trovera
Tiene seis cuerdas de alambre
Para cantar donde quiera
Lo de aquel tiempo de hambre

My father, mother, aunts, uncles, etc., grew up in the middle of this scenario of famine and chaos. As a father and grandfather, I cannot fathom the anguish of my grandfather for his motherless young family. What options does a widower campesino have to be able to provide not only daily needs but also to develop hopes for the future.

God bless America, or at least the State of California.

So Don Cipriano Barbosa, in one swift and daring gamble, moved to the state of California with all six children in tow. They established a family outpost in the town of Van Nuys. His first cousin Narciso Fernandez had a small produce ranch in the area and helped Don Cipriano learn the ropes. This happened, as best we can tell, during the early 1920s. To this day, descendants of Narciso and Josefa Fernandez are deeply rooted in this area. For example, Pastor Sam Meza Jr. with the Sepulveda Christian Center continues to carry on this family's tradition of service and community work.

In this then-small farming community, the Barbosa men found work in nearby farms. Some, however, had to go as far south as Escondido. They picked up English quickly, compared to many of the people I know who came to the US when I did. To this day, many of them still struggle with English.

The Barbosa men were semi-itinerant workers. Still, they would cultivate fruits and vegetables at their own small farm and keep small farm animals. Folks in the vicinity would come to the Barbosa's to buy eggs, honey, fruits, vegetables, and other products. The Barbosa girls were in charge of this small but important cash stream.

Maria de la Paz had recently turned twenty, the story goes, and a young man began courting her in earnest. He did not meet with the approval of my grandfather, however. Looking for a way to cool the romance, my grandfather decided to send Maria de la Paz to spend some time with cousin Jesus Trejo's family back in Monterrey, Mexico.

Ah, the Mexico of the 1920s! The wounds of the revolution were still fresh. Instead of bringing troops, arms, and destruction, however, the trains of Ferrocarriles Nacionales de Mexico now brought the chimeric promise of a new beginning. Hope rang out like the lugubrious train whistle. The hustle and bustle of the stations, the calls of vendors hawking their goods, the rich smells of foods full of herbs and spices, the melee of music, from traditional to tribal…I have this romantic idea that this was the scene when Maria de la Paz and Emilio met.

So Maria de la Paz Barbosa traveled by train to the dynamic, industrial city of Monterrey, Mexico, to be with her cousins in the Trejo family.

> Esta tarde a Modesta encontré
> Por las calles lúcidas de Iguala
> Y me dijo me vine a pasear
> En un tren desde Tetecala

We don't know the exact circumstances under which Maria de la Paz and Emilio met. Of course, we can assume they met in Monterrey. Passion took hold of Maria de la Paz in Monterrey, and Van Nuys kept drifting further and further into the distance.

By this time in the romance, Don Cipriano Barbosa was already back in Lerdo, Durango. We do not know why. This was the late 1920s, and the government was likely spreading the word about fulfilling the revolutionary promises of Tierra y Libertad—the ideal of the hero Emiliano Zapata. In fact, Zapata was reportedly one of Che Guevara's earliest heroes.

Don Cipriano wanted to be ready for when the so-called farmland reformation and distribution took place. So he was running a "split household"—if Tios Enrique and Cipriano were not with him in Lerdo at this time, they would be joining him soon, leaving Tio Juan and Tias Lupe and Josefina running the Van Nuys frontline. Don Cipriano's presence in Lerdo could also have been due to his concern for his daughter and her new romance. By all appearances, the entire family adored Maria de la Paz. When Tio Juan or Tio Cipriano talked with family and friends, they would refer to her as Paz mi Hermana. Even many years later, their affection was still apparent.

So Maria de la Paz invites Emilio to Lerdo to meet her father.

> Por las señas que te voy a dar
> En mi casa puedes encontrar
> En la puerta un barandal de acero
> Y un letrero de Modesta Ayala
>
> Otro día por tierra me fui
> Muy temprano llegué a Tetecala
> Lo primero que voy encontrando
> Y un letrero de Modesta Ayala
>
> Ella misma le habló a su padre
> Con muchísima amabilidad
> Allí está un hombre que busca trabajo
> Usted dice Papá si le da
>
> Soy un hombre que viene de lejos
> Vivo errante como un vagabundo
> Mi camisa es de manta rayada
> Mis huaraches de tres agujeros.
>
> Con tres días que estuve en la casa
> Ella a mí me robó la existencia
> Y Modesta ha de ser mi mujer
> Mientras Dios me conceda licencia

They married on October 4, 1929, at 10:00 p.m. They were united in matrimony by Jose Garcia Gutierrez, civil judge and mayor of Ciudad Lerdo, Durango, Mexico. Serving as one of the witnesses was Don Cipriano Barbosa.

Don Cipriano did not like the suitor Paz had in Van Nuys, and we have no reason to believe he would have liked Emilio either. Paz loved Emilio; therefore, Don Cipriano loved Emilio. This scenario between Emilio and Paz reminds me of the struggle between Flavia and Sergio 60 plus years later. In every aspect, they are one and the same.

Don Cipriano's next move was the result of a great deal of thought and calculation. The brand new Briones collective set up shop in Monterrey. One clearly understands Don Cipriano's predicament. Just as he probably silently predicted, it was not a bed of roses for the newly formed Briones household. It was not that Paz was out of her element, as a naive farm girl suddenly in the city. It was not Paz's realization that Emilio was condemned to work for the rest of his life at the factory without hope of advancement. It was not the two unsuccessful pregnancies she had suffered. Don Cipriano was frustrated; he knew the root of their problems but could not help them fix it and give them a chance of a happy life together.

Paz and Emilio are deeply incompatible. Just like Flavia and Sergio, they conversed in the same language, but one may as well have been speaking Greek and the other Chinese. In the personality quadrant—driver, analytical, expressive, passive—these four—Emilio, Sergio, Paz, and Flavia—are top heavy with expressive/passive traits. (It's worth noting that "expressive" as used in the personality quadrant does not necessarily mean having a gift for explanations.) The existence of a combination of expressive/passive traits in excess often results in an individual being easily angered or their feelings easily hurt. That makes him/her excessively volatile, aggressively or passively.

This is what my grandfather Don Cipriano and I were contemplating. Here are these four products of their respective environments that bring to the table their immense needs. Among them, I counted their need to be nurtured. The irony is that what humans most need to hear is what they are less capable or willing to declare: their mutual needs.

They have to come to understand they have legitimate needs and that they do have the capacity to help each other. They have to learn to nurture.

In Don Cipriano's case, probably just as in mine, in all of the conversations I ever witnessed between Flavia and Sergio—happy, angry and everything in between—I do not remember a single one in which either one of ever fully understood what the other meant. Before I go any further, I should clarify, this is not meant as a criticism of my mother, father, Flavia or Sergio. This is meant to show how Mother Nature specifically designed us to royally screw ourselves. Emilio Noir and I agree that this is Mother Nature's Kobayashi Maru.

So here we have these four in the middle of yet another Kobayashi Maru.

Critical issues in relationships: So if in the relationship before you, you have a critical issue, one that can make or break you, because you are easily angered or your feelings easily hurt, it is very unlikely that you will be able to properly communicate where you are in this issue. And because the other side is also easily angered/hurt, it is also unlikely that you will be able to understand the other side of it. In the case of these four, it is a double whammy. All four are in the same emotionally critical plane. Communications do not quite come out right, nor are received the way they are meant. So, *all* the decisions and actions made by individuals operating from this base are triggered by instinct (and fear).

Operating solely by instinct is like going to a casino and playing slot machines: you might win now and then, but the odds are against you. The American psychologist and philosopher William James said, "There is no worse lie than a truth misunderstood by those who hear it." This, my friend, is a Kobayashi Maru scenario *in all its glory*. And this is what Don Cipriano and I sensed in terms of their future together. To want to explain the mechanics of this to my dear father, mother, daughter or son-in-law so they can have some type of chance together, is like wanting to make apple pie using Carl Sagan's recipe: To make apple pie from scratch, you first have to create a universe.

What do you do? What can you do? One cannot just stand and watch! Even if you do nothing—doing nothing is still an action— the stress will still get you. Maybe one can go against one's better judgment and against the Federation of Planets Prime Directive. My grandfather understood it was not his decision to make or his place to interfere. Still, Don Cipriano decides to take Emilio out of his environment and, therefore, out of his comfort zone and bring him in into the Barbosa collective. Even though, Don Cipriano and I believe that with this decision their future has a better chance, we know it is not our decision to make, and we believe, right or wrong, that we will forever be responsible for what happens to that person as a result of this decision.

ENRIQUE BARBOSA

Under Don Cipriano's suggestion, Emilio relocates to Lerdo and begins a new life with Paz under the Barbosa umbrella. I believe during this time, Tio Enrique has been quite the busy camper. He has been back to Lerdo from Van Nuys, married Felicitas, probably had two kids with her and was now farming and running some type of transport service to the neighboring rural areas.

> Y por esa calle vive
> La que a mí me abandonó
> Su mamá tuvo la culpa
> Pues ella se lo ordenó

Tio Cipriano, a busy camper himself, married back in Van Nuys. As was common in those days, Tio Cipriano's father and mother in-law were very involved and critical of their personal life to the point where they gave her the ultimatum of choosing between them and Tio Cipriano. She chose the parents. This is quite the love story. She died a couple of years after this took place; the rumors of the day were that she was lovesick. Divorced and disillusioned, Tío Cipriano makes his come back to Lerdo.

> Negra, Negra consentida
> Negra de mi vida
> Quién te quiere a ti?

During this new Lerdo period, and after the two failed pregnancies in Monterrey, Paz has given birth to Josefina (my sister), who was given the nickname Negra and will herein be referred to as Neg, and to Cipriano Briones (my brother), who was given the nickname Prieto and herein referred to as Cip.

The Obregón Period

> Sonora querida tierra consentida
> De dicha y placer
> Cajeme tan rico donde hasta
> El más chico tiene su tostón

Neg was born on April 8, 1933; Cip was born on July 5, 1935 (both in Lerdo, Durango). He was six months old when the Briones clan relocated to Cajeme (Obregón), Sonora.

The Barbosas had escaped the mass deportation of Mexicans from the United States during the 1930s for two reasons (and luck): One, when bringing everybody to California, Don Cipriano had the foresight and due diligence to process everybody's documents and bring them to the USA legally; and two, they had picked up the language, so they had a chance of defending themselves by showing they were in the country legally if confronted. This was important because many Mexican families, even many Mexicans who were US citizens, were still deported to Mexico. This is exactly what happened to Cundi and his mother, aunts, uncles, cousins, etc. The Coss family was deported and settled in Nogales and Hermosillo. Eventually after a few years, they proved their citizenship and found their way back to the USA. Meanwhile, the Barbosas were able to come and go freely from California to Lerdo to Obregón, etc.

The Barbosa and Briones clans are now in Obregón. Don Cipriano (my grandfather) managed to get some farmland. We do not know the circumstances. We do not know if he bought it or borrowed it from a landowner or agrarista or if he himself was in the agrarista program.

> Voy a contar un corrido
> De un amigo de mi tierra
> Llamándose Valentin
> Que fue fusilado
> Y colgado en la sierra

After the revolution, "Los Cristeros" was the last popular rebellion in the twentieth century in Mexico, though some would say the last real revolution was when the PAN's Vicente Fox won the presidency, ending seventy years of PRI one-party rule. During this struggle, thousands of peasants sided with the Catholic church against the state and its agrarian reform program, or as it is referred to in Mexico, Los Agraristas.

> Al llegar al paredón
> Valentín quiso llorar
> Madre mía de Guadalupe
> Por tu religión
> Me van a matar

This reformation sought to "as a matter of law, conserve their communal character, to have legal capacity to enjoy in common the waters, woods, and lands belonging to them, or which may have been or shall be restored to them according to the law of January 6, 1915, until such time, as the manner of making the division of lands shall be determined by law."

It would be easy for the casual observer to deduce two aspects here. The state is clearly facing a dilemma: they won the revolution but have no plan to govern. The state also wants to appear to be making amends to the Mexican lower classes for the injustices suffered at the hands of the previous government. All they have to give at this point is land and the hope it carries for a better life. One can guess the degree of corruption and outrage when peasants who were supposed to benefit from agrarian reform rise up and take arms against it. The cost in terms of lives and the government's credibility was incredible. Agrarian reform remains an open wound in Mexico, as families that ended up with the best lands have become fabulously wealthy as agribusiness flourished. I would not be surprised if most of the land ended up back in the hands of the land barons from whom they were taken.

Meanwhile back at the farm, I know it was a struggle, and the odds were against the clan. Campesinos who got land were the exception. Campesinos who then managed to hold on to that land were a downright anomaly. The infrastructure or lack thereof was not conducive to small farming.

To make ends meet while farming, Tio Enrique (in Obregón now) got at a full-time job in a lumberyard. At the same time, he continued to take on more work...and more family. By now we had a new aunt, Tia Margarita, and a new cousin, Enriquito. I hear that Tio Cipriano for a time had the contract to deliver the mail to some of the rural towns in the Altar Valley. He supplemented his income by selling sundries to the people in the different towns and hamlets along his route. Emilio Briones set up a makeshift carpentry shop where he did odd jobs. I vaguely remember one time when he was making a coffin. He also had a horse and flatbed buggy, which he used to deliver packages from the railroad depot to people all over town. He even delivered the movie reels to the local open-air movie houses.

During this period, the economic differences between Mexico and the Western United States were not so obvious, at least not to a Mexican in the United States with the dream of owning his own business. Juan Barboza (Uncle Juan), his home in Van Nuys, by now had married Helenita and had four daughters: Dolores, Lucilla, Lucy and Josefina. So Tio Juan *quema las naves* (burns the bridges), selling everything, uprooting his family and heading south to Sonora.

Left in Van Nuys was Tia Lupe, who by now had married Margarito Reyes and had Nena, Lalo, Beto, Lonny and Lina. Tia Josefina had married Santiago Canales and would eventually have Carmen, Esperanza, Juan, Josefina, Miguel, Santiago, Rita, Enrique, Maria and Luis. Tio Cipriano married Belen and now lived in Atil, Sonora. He would remain there until his death in December of 1998.

Taken early 1941, just before Don Cipriano left California for the last time to go to Obregón, is probably the last photo taken of him

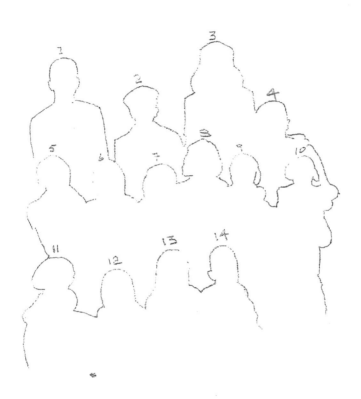

1. Eddie Reyes
2. Beto Reyes
3. Nena Reyes
4. Don Cipriano Barbosa
5. Loni Reyes
6. Dolores Barbosa
7. Esperanza Canales
8. Carmen Canales
9. Josefina Canales
10. Josefina Barbosa
11. Lina Reyes
12. Sylvia Barbosa
13. Lucy Barbosa
14. Juan Canales

In these photos taken April 1941, Neg is 8,
Cip 5 and I am "3 meses, 25 dias"
The lady is "Nacha" my godmother.
These photos were taken on occasion of my baptism.

the cousings 70 years later

The plan called for Juan to relocate to Obregón, strengthen the collective by consolidating the numbers of family members, insist on the farm dream and start a business, specifically a *molino* (a mill). It was a great concept; people in the neighborhood now would have a place to bring their corn to be ground. This molino would also have a *tortillería*.

I remember my father saying the molino was working great, for a while. Uncle Juan was a tall, handsome, distinguished man. The viejas in the neighborhood, it seemed, always had a reason for fluttering around the molino. According to my father, Tia Helenita didn't take kindly to this.

On February 13, 1944, Maria de la Paz Briones Barbosa died giving birth to a son, Francisco Javier. Dr. Ramos, whose daughter Elsa had Del Bac build her a house in Tucson fifty-seven years later, was the attending physician. From here on, until almost the end of his life, Emilio Briones Yglesias would not have anything to do with doctors. There were only two types of people on his persona non grata list: the mainstream medical profession (the industry) and organized religion.

When news of Maria de la Paz's death reached the uncles and cousins in California, Tia Lupe and cousin Helen made the trip to be with us a few days. This photo of the cousins was taken at this time. Neg is the tall one in back. To her left is Dolores, and to her right is Sylvia. The adult in the center is cousin Helen Reyes. To Helen's left is Lucy; to Helen's right is Josefina. Dolores, Lucy, Sylvia and Josefina being the Barboza girls. I'm the one in front of Helen.

MARIA DE LA PAZ

Neg was 10 years and nine months old. Cip was eight years and seven months old. Having been born on Christmas day 1940, I was three.

With the death of my mother, and the birth of my brother Francisco Javier, my father and my grandfather had a number of challenges. Among them, who's going to take care of the newborn. Neg was already facing the impossible to imagine challenge of, at ten years old, having to take over the Briones's household duties, including being a mother to Cip and I. So it was either Tio Juan's household or Tio Enrique's.

Tio Juan and Tio Enrique were immersed up to their armpits in their own Kobayashi Maru. This must have been obvious to my grandfather and father. So, perhaps with little deliberation to do, Francisco Javier was turned over to Tio Juan.

My mother's death was the beginning of the end of the Barbosa's Obregón period. It was also the beginning of the end of my grandfather's dreams (for the collective) and, therefore, the beginning of the end of his life.

My brother Francisco Javier, as the most vulnerable with the least defense, is at the bottom of the food chain.

In his home "de jour," Tio Juan's household, you would find, for example, the Barbosa girls, in a strangely different setting, surrounded by strange people behaving strangely. Even the familiar faces were different, hostile, loud, always fighting. It was of no consequence that the adults' behavior was justifiable considering all the things going on, including my mother's tragic death.

Tia Elenita (Tio Juan's wife) was also upon hard times. Uprooted from her home in California, she landed in the middle of a crisis, far away from the security net and the moral support of her side of the family, with no friends. She is having to start a household, and (whether she wanted to or not) be a mother to a baby that was not hers, chase away female clients from the molino and Tio Juan, who was now seen as "fair game" by the *viejas* in the neighborhood. The list of preoccupations on her plate goes on and on.

JUAN BARBOSA

As head of the household, Tio Juan was up to his armpits in alligators! By now he is learning first-hand the sobering lesson we all learn but quickly forget, that things are never as they appear. The Mexico he remembered from his youth was not the way he remembered it. In fact, he now realized that it was really never as he thought it was. Nostalgia is a powerful and often hallucinogenic drug. They say you can cure nostalgia for an old girlfriend by getting to know her again. In short order, you will be reminded of why the relationship didn't last.

Tio Juan is frustrated. No matter how hard he tries, his security blanket is simply not large enough to cover everybody pulling at the edges all at the same time. His frustrations are aggravated by the crash course in corruption he is getting courtesy of the Mexican government. Small businesses are especially vulnerable, he is discovering. Alligators are everywhere.

At this moment in Tio Juan's household, my grandfather drops by to visit. He finds Francisco Javier in bad conditions. He realizes he must remove the baby from the house. He and my father take him to Tio Enrique and turn him over to his care.

For Francisco Javier, it turns out that this is not an upgrade. Or maybe it was already too late. One could make the case that Tio Enrique's alligators were bigger and hungrier than Tio Juan's. For Tio Juan, even though it is not easy, all he has to do is buy train tickets for everybody and go back to the US. Tio Enrique has already gone through the same trauma Tio Juan is going through at this time. But Tio Enrique does not have anything to sell to be able to go look for greener pastures, or he might be thinking he can still make it work.

Francisco Javier died in July 1944. Perhaps this was Tio Juan's cue to pack things up and move back to the US. With no time to waste, he left it all—the business, the miscellaneous mill and tortillería equipment, the home he had bought on Calle Jardín etc.—all in the hands of my grandfather. He left instructions to sell everything as soon as possible, liquidate payables and forward whatever money was left to him in the US. This was not an easy task for my grandfather, in light of the economic depression in the US and Mexico.

In July of the following year, Tio Enrique died in a freak accident at his job at the lumberyard. While cutting a timber, the blade in the bench saw got stuck and kicked the timber back. The timber hit him in the heart and killed him. At the time, his wife Tia Margarita was pregnant with cousin Leticia.

With the trauma of these three deaths so close together, my grandfather Don Cipriano barely had enough life left in him to liquidate Tio Juan's belongings, pay what was owed and send him the leftover money. He also traveled to Hermosillo to negotiate an indemnification from Tio Enrique's employer on behalf of the widow and her son Manuel Enrique and daughter Leticia, so they could relocate some place where they could find a support system of their own.

CIPRIANO BARBOSA

Tio Cipriano lived with his wife Belen in the hamlet of Atil, Sonora, near the town of Caborca. He came to Obregón and took my grandfather with him to Atil. Before my grandfather left Obregón, he had tombstones made for Francisco Javier, Enrique and Maria de la Paz. I remember visiting these tombs during Día de los Muertos. I am not sure, but I believe years later Cip sent money to Obregón to have a tumba remade for Francisco Javier. My mother died in

February 1944; Francisco Javier died in July 1944; Tio Enrique died in July 1945; and Don Cipriano died in Atil in December 1945.

We were dropping like flies. Before Neg could blink an eye, everyone had disappeared. There was no one left except us pollitos, little chickens.

> Juan se llamaba
> Y lo apodaban
> Charrasqueado
> Era atrevido y arriesgado
> En el amor
> A las muchachas más bonitas
> Se llevaba
> En aquellos campos
> No quedaba
> Ni una flor

People living in poverty have always been at the bottom of the bottom rung of not only the food chain, but also the scales of justice in Mexico. The cancer of corruption in the Mexican government, together with the poverty of the people, bred violence, insecurity and injustice. Obregón of the 1940s was just like anywhere else in Mexico, the land and culture that helped coin the term *macho*.

Any man in any position of authority could, and often would, abduct any defenseless female they wished. Poor women were defenseless with no real rights or means of defending themselves in a nation where their worst enemy is—even today—the government.

These macho men usually fit the same profile: middle-aged with at least one household (an existing wife or lover), several kids, works in some government job with some authority, however minimal (municipal, state, etc.). Up until now, this predator needed a horse. In the forties, however, he needed a car. But he doesn't have to own the car; he can borrow a government car for a few days.

Usually, girls were plucked from small towns and often taken somewhere far away, where her shame could be kept a secret and he could continue to exert control over her.

Zenon Veliz was such a villain. I believe he worked for the municipio, probably as a mechanic. Normally, this would place him barely above campesino class. I do not know how many kids he had. I met one of them when he was a teenager. His name was Museo. Wow! What names! Zenon kidnapped Neg early in the second half of 1945. Zenon, you bastard! She was twelve and a half years old! Your son was older than she!

Zenon did not care that Neg's mother died recently, her brother shortly thereafter and her uncle just a few days before. Is that vulnerable enough for you, you Godless coward? Usually I try not to judge, but I am judging him to hell right here.

Of course, Zenon's actions are an extreme manifestation of a Mexican archetype. This extreme aspect is glorified and brought to the status of hero by various popular Mexican songs and movies of the 1940s and 50s.

There was talk in the neighborhood that it was some kind of bet he had made. He was going to do it because he could. He took her to Nogales, Sonora. He kept her there a few weeks in the house of a sister. Nogales might as well have been Mars! I remember years later when I went to Nogales for the first time. What a strange place, adults wear shoes instead of huaraches, and kids like me, they wear them too instead of going barefoot! The streets have this hard surface called pavement. I also got a chance to experience up close and personal, for the first time, this wondrous thing called electricity!

As of this writing, no one is alive that was an adult (young or otherwise) during this period. There is no one to help me recall the specifics.

We are now in 1946. It is time for Zenon to get back to Obregón. Neg was already pregnant with Juan. I want to think Zenon's capacity for empathy finally kicked in and he brings Neg back to our household (instead of just abandoning her in Nogales) and tells my father he's going to marry Neg and move in. We did not know at the time that he was already married, had a wife and at least one son. In Mexican culture, Neg and Zenon's household is called *la casa chica*—the little house.

With Neg back home, Prieto and I had our mother back!

30

Life went on… Neg at 13 had a "husband" and was a pregnant mother of two. Prieto was 11, and I was six years old. For Neg, there were no support systems on site other than ourselves. Nevertheless, we were now all together again. We were growing up in double jeopardy: orphans in Mexico.

Juan is born on June 30, 1947. His birth certificate reads Juan Manuel Veliz Briones (6-30-47/5-22-98). Neg had turned 14 just two months earlier.

In mid-1948, when Juan was almost a year old, Zenon ran off with some girl. We believe she was an "older" one this time. He lived with her in another part of town. We don't know how long this relationship lasted. We do know that he had another family with her. There were at least two more women after her—each one being stranded with children—then we lost track of his depravity.

About this time, Don Emilio had gotten Prieto a job at the Hotel Colonial, the best in town at this time. He probably started as a *mandadero* and luggage carrier, or *botones*.

CIPRIANO BRIONES

Hotel Colonial Cd. Obregon, Son. Mex

At the tender age of 12, he had a better job than many adults in our neighborhood. He had managed to make it to the third grade—even with all the tumult and drama in our lives—before being forced to start his life as a worker.

It was now the middle of 1950. Neg and three-year-old Juan are on their way to Van Nuys, California to stay with Tia Lupe. At Tia Lupe and Tio Juan's suggestion, the plan was to process Neg and Juan's documents so they could relocate to the US. I believe Tio Juan was acting as the sponsor. The legalization process was carried all the way to the point at which only one final item was needed: consent from Juan's father. The document was drafted and made ready for Zenon's signature. Neg and Juan traveled back to Obregón to ask Zenon for his signature.

In early 1951, Neg was back with us while she was finding Zenon to go through the humbling exercise of asking him for his signature. His response was more than a despotic "no"; it was an emphatic "Hell no!" My second judgment: what an ignorant son of a bitch!

Neg & Juan at the time she came back to Obregón,
seeking an audience with Zenon

All of those badly needed resources used to process the documentation, traveling back and forth, going to the different Mexican government agencies that extracted *mordidas* for documents they are entitled to receive for free…all of this just so the one item that would naturally be the easiest to obtain would be denied. This would surely take the wind out of the most stoic person's sails.

So back to square one for Neg and Juan. In early 1952, Neg was 19. It is difficult to assess the level of intellectual understanding and, therefore, the capacity a 19-year-old in this situation would have in terms figuring out her next step. Even though as humans we are capable of adapting to tremendous change, we remain victims of habit. Clear decisions are often clouded by false promises, be they of comfort, routine, conformity or nostalgia.

With the US option now closed and despair taking a hold, Neg retreated to the tribe. Prieto and I triggered an instinctual reaction in her to stay with the status quo, to stay in Obregón and take care of us. After all, this option provides the security of a roof for over both of their heads. She had the sympathy and goodwill of the neighbors, who would surely lend a hand up to the limits of their purse strings. She had friends: Esther Navarro; her husband, Antonio Navarro; and Esther's mother, Dona Rosa Soto de Soqui.

I remember an anecdote from those days that captures the times: I was outside playing in the dirt, making mud toys (the dirt must have had a high clay content because when mixed with water and brought to the right texture, it felt like Play-Doh). All of a sudden, Dona Rosa started running back and forth, looking up and pointing to the sky as she shouted, "The world is coming to an end! The world is coming to an end! O dear Jesus, have mercy on us!" Then, in the middle of the street, she knelt and, with her arms open, began to pray. It turned out that it was a sky-writing airplane starting to write an ad in the sky. The ad was "Drink Pepsi Cola." What can I tell you? Perhaps we were not so up to date those days in Obregón—maybe just a few years (decades?) behind the times.

As if all of this were not enough to cloud Neg's mind, a cultural element also weighed heavily in the decision-making process. This scenario is by no means exclusive to Neg or to Mexico. Many had faced it before, and many will face it again. There was (maybe still is, at certain levels and in certain circles in Mexico) an unwritten rule that was not open for debate: the death of the mother automatically put the oldest daughter in charge of the household. She will be in charge and unable to have a personal life until all her younger siblings are adults, or the father remarries. When the father is the one who dies, the responsibility falls on the oldest brother. So, there was a powerful precedent for Neg to heed.

No one could possibly have known the tremendous responsibility and ramifications of the decision Neg was facing. Her next move is what cemented and shaped the lives of Cipriano, Juan and me.

She decided to ignore the local wisdom of the time and face the unknown. She decided to take the road less traveled. It is a decision for which Juan, Cipriano and I will always be grateful. In a tremendous show of courage and self-assurance, she and Juan moved

34

to Nogales, Sonora, to make way for Cip and I to follow to start a new life.

Time and space played a major subliminal role in preparing Neg as they (time and space) brought her to this juncture. Events began to run together, or time stood still as events passed.

My mother dies in February of 1944. My grandfather Don Cipriano Barbosa dies in December 1945. In the middle, Tio Juan's lifelong dreams and possessions quickly evaporate before his eyes, and he has to relocate twice, etc. Tio Enrique's life-changing events during this short period have a far-reaching impact. Don Cipriano Barbosa has a number of things to get done, including arranging the funeral of his daughter. He is just barely drying his eyes, and he has to bury his grandson. A few months later, he arranges the funeral of his son Enrique. He senses his time is rapidly running out. In between funerals, he manages to sell the property and equipment left by Tio Juan and pay outstanding bills.

We are now approaching the end of 1945. He still wants to tidy up a few things, such as the legal aspects of the deaths. He commissions grave markers for his son and daughter. But most importantly, he travels back and forth to the Sonoran capital of Hermosillo to negotiate an indemnification settlement with the company that employed Tio Enrique. Despite the tight timeframe, he was successful in getting the indemnification.

Even nowadays in Mexico, things generally do not move this fast. Time stood still to allow Don Cipriano to get all these things done. It was as if life owed him that much in the end.

Tia Margarita had the indemnification money in hand, a running start toward new horizons. My grandfather can now comfortably close the book on his life. In the end, he did not even want to burden the Briones with another funeral. He had his son Cipriano come to Obregón and take him to his home in Atil, Sonora, where he spent his final days in December of 1945.

The Nogales Period

At 19, Neg decided to pick up stakes and relocate to Nogales, Sonora, with Juan.

The way of life in a "cesspool" border town like Nogales was a tremendous contrast compared to the clean and simple life in a town like Obregón. Of course, good heroic people are everywhere, and thankfully in greater numbers than malicious people. The problem with the Nogaleses of the world is that they force people to change to survive: people have to become ruthless; they have no limits as to whom they hurt or how or why or over how much. This was true then, just as it is today. Borders are places where hard decisions are made every minute. Worlds collide, and people get banged up in the process.

In early 1952, Neg was establishing a precarious foothold in Nogales. Later that year, Cip followed. He had experience working in a hotel, so he found employment at the then-prestigious Marcos de Niza Hotel.

A year later on November 20, 1953, I arrived to join them in Nogales. I was not yet 13. Many basic things were beyond my worldview.

I remember leaving Obregón more than arriving to Nogales. My midnight escape broke my father's heart. We were the only things he had. Like most kids, I quit school after the fifth grade to help the household in any way possible. So my father and I worked and did everything together. At the train depot, everybody had a nickname. His was *culatas* (the butt of a rifle), so everybody called me *culatitas*.

Left to right, Chuy, Juan in the arms of Cip and Don Emilio,
that's one of two horses we had, I don't remember it's name.
This is the carreta used to deliver packages to and from the train depot, to
various merchants in town, including the local cinema houses in town.

There was a strong bond of endearment. Men of my father's era and background, the ration of tenderness, given them at birth, by nature, buried way down deep and not allowed to surface by the harshness of their environment, would be hard to understand today. Hard to understand would be the dreaded machete he kept behind the door. He would use the side of the machete on our backs (Neg's, Cip's or mine) to discipline us—more often on Cip. The machete marks on Cip's back would last for months. Like the time when Cip got paid for the first time at the Hotel Colonial. He went straight to the mercado and bought towels, toothpaste and toothbrushes for everyone. Cip's action was punished with the machete. The marks of the machete on Cip's back were deep, but not as deep as the scars on Cip's psyche. Incredible! In spite of all this, I always felt a strong tender connection with my father.

Yet at the blink of an eye (not 13 years old yet), I abandoned him when the opportunity came. Perhaps at some level I understood that this was inevitable. It had to happen, so better sooner than later.

Neg worked at a tortillería, which is where she met Cundi and shortly thereafter set up a one-room household. There we all lived: Juan, Cundi's mother, Dona Catalina, Cip (who worked at the Fray Marcos de Niza) and me (I worked the streets).

JUAN COSS

Cundi (Secundino 12-6-1920/10-20-2003) had recently relocated from the city of Hermosillo to Nogales to have his status as a US citizen reinstated. He and his mother and siblings had been deported during the mass deportations of the 1930s. He worked in Nogales, Arizona, as a day laborer.

Shortly after arriving in Nogales, I hooked up with a kid about my age in the same neighborhood. Luis was streetwise. He taught me the rules of survival. We washed cars, sold newspapers and lottery tickets (like the kid that sells a lottery ticket to Humphrey Bogart in the movie *The Treasure of the Sierra Madre*), shined shoes and, most importantly, stayed one step ahead of Agapito. Agapito was the security guard paid by the downtown merchants to keep the riffraff away from the tourists. I quickly graduated to the next level by making a connection with a guy who supplied street vendors with *joyería de fantasia* ("fantasy jewelry") also known as *chafa* (something lousy or of bad quality) for the tourist market. Thinking back, I don't know if tourists bought my chafa out of pity or because I would not take no for an answer. Of course, this automatically placed me in a more prominent place on Agapito's persona non grata list.

It was this distributor of chafa who, wanting to show me an alternative market for the product, took me to La Canal. La Canal is the red-light district in Nogales. Prostitution was legal at the time in Mexico, as it still is. Pimping is illegal now. Working girls had to be registered with the Municipal Government, carry an ID and be certified as disease free by the health department. But the women had to live at a residence of record provided by their employer. They also could not stray outside of the "official" perimeter of the red-light district. They could roam the city freely only one day a week: "health department" day. Any girl caught outside of the district would quickly be picked up, fined and returned to her "house" of record. This sequestration made them easy prey to street vendors. For this and some other reasons, the house owners had tough restrictions as to who had access to these houses.

The chafa dealer (I don't remember his name) had an "in" with one of the girls, so we were allowed to go in and visit her at her house. What little inventory I had sold quickly, but we still stayed the whole afternoon because they had not seen each other in a while and wanted to "catch up." What I saw that afternoon depressed me. I looked into a depressing world in which no one there was who they thought they would end up being in life. On the way back to town, he said now that I knew how to get in, I could go there on slow days. I'm sure I went back several times, even though I don't remember that, or remember slow days.

By 1954, Cip had been working at the Marcos de Niza for about a year. Life in Nogales was tough and not getting easier. He decided to move to the port of Mazatlán. Life there certainly could not be worse than Nogales, or so he thought.

Neg continues to work at the tortillería while Juan attended school at Escuela Pestalozi. Cundi's style of drunkenness made Neg's life with him a living hell.

Emilio Briones's resilience led him to the wise decision of finding Anita Morales and bringing her into his life by marrying her and starting a new life and family. Anita already had a daughter, Chuyita. My brother Sergio would be born from this union.

While in the streets, I am "discovered" by Jose Silva. Jose is a *cobijero*. He offers me a job as his cargador, or carrier (like a mule). *Cobijero* is a pejorative term for a door-to-door salesman. Cobijeros would trek through neighborhoods selling different wares, including cobijas (blankets), clothing, irons, radios, etc. He would load me up with inventory, and my job was to follow him.

Every day we would walk the town of Nogales in its entirety, all the hills, all the neighborhoods. At the end of the workday, we would walk back to the place that was supplying him with the inventory. The place was the Sonora Electric, property of Jesus Cano and his partner from the US, Mr. Goldsmith. After we turned in the inventory in to Sonora Electric, Jose would pay me for the daytime portion of my job. Jose also rented a small floor area space inside of one of the *cantinas de mala muerte*, a bad bar in a bad part of town. In this space, he set up a wood burning stove and a *cocinera*. The cocinera made and sold tacos to the *borrachos*. My nighttime job with Jose was to keep the cocinera company and run errands. My salary for this part of my job included a full order (3) of tacos. Because Jose would go home at the beginning of the evening, and I would not see him again until the next day at Sonora Electrica, he would pay me for the evening in advance.

For a moment during the day, I would have the money from the day's work, plus the money in advance for the evening's work. Jose would go home for the evening, and the cocinera was busy making the order of tacos for me as part of my payment. She knew that I was forever hungry. Her tacos were great, and she knew that before the evening was over, I would spend all of my wages on her tacos. At the end of the night at closing, she would serve me more tacos on the house. So I would be walking home at midnight or one in the morning and see this old man (I don't remember his name even though we became friendly) by the sidewalk selling *pan de dulce* (Mexican sweet bread). Still hungry, I would talk him into selling me bread on credit. Ah the bliss of ignorance! At the end of a hell of a long day, working my tail to the bone, I would end up in the hole because I ate more than I made. But I don't remember ever being tired or ever being unhappy. I only remember never having enough tacos! Forty, fifty years later, Emilio Noir and I were running an errand in Nogales, Sonora, saw a young man that reminded us of this period, I'll tell you more at another time, since I don't want to digress too far.

I often wondered how I would explain this level of poverty to somebody from the Midwest, for example. I say the Midwest because I have great respect and admiration for such people. Among those I have had the privilege of knowing (such as Bob Ott, originally from Michigan, we worked side by side, for more than 30 years), they seem to have a common goodness: honest, fair, hard-working, always willing to do that extra something. So if I say to someone from there that I am poor, he/she would surely reply by asking, "So why the hell don't you have a job? Are you afraid of hard work?" For somebody born and raised in the US—where in the 1940s and 50s US industry was a global powerhouse with dynamic growth and opportunities that helped create the world's largest and most prosperous middle class—it can be hard to understand the realities of Mexico.

In Mexico, individuals could not move mountains in the same way as in the United States. Corruption and money were the rule of law; they still are. And when they didn't work, violence was the judge and jury. How do you explain that to someone who comes from a place where elected officials largely do their job, where corruption is the exception, not the rule? No one can conceptualize it without living it.

It was the beginning of 1955 now. Cip had relocated to Guadalajara—an indication that Mazatlán was not a picnic. Neg's life with Cundi, from where I sat, continued to be hell on earth. In her early days in Nogales, she met a beautiful soul in the person of Raquel Avechuco Soto de Bueno.

RAQUEL

God allowed their paths to cross, and they became friends. Raquel and her compassion were a great source of much-needed moral support. They were like sisters. Their alliance will last lifetimes beyond this world. Raquel's children at this time were Raul, Gloria and Gildardo. She would reconcile with her husband Gildardo Bueno, move back to Cananea and eventually have Frida, Palmiro, Vladimir, Pancho and Patty before meeting an untimely death in a freak car accident in Cananea.

Meanwhile back in the streets of Nogales…

One morning I went to Sonora Electric to start another work-day, and Jose told me he had to go check something out first and to follow him. We would return later, he told me. There was a guy from Guadalajara in town interviewing people to sell door-to-door. His name was Mr. Rodriguez. I don't remember his first name, even though I got to know him well. I was Jose's shadow, ever-present during the interview. Mr. Rodriguez was tall and slim with a fair complexion. He was well-dressed with elegant manners, and he spoke Spanish like I had never heard it before, the way it was meant to be spoken (and would never hear it again, until I heard the silky ambrosia-like Spanish of Eric Healy, perhaps the finest handball player I ever met, or so he keeps telling me). By the end of my experience with Rodriguez, I would speak Spanish as well as he did.

Rodriguez agreed to take Jose out in the field for a one-time tryout with a real client to show him what he called the "argument." The argument was a sales script he designed for all his salespeople to use with prospective clients. Rodriguez was in the business of manufacturing and selling 12-inch by 12-inch framed images of the Virgin of Fátima. She was very popular at that time among Catholics, especially in Mexico.

Rodriguez started out the "tour" in Guadalajara and made his way north one town and city at the time, all the way to Nogales. His current group consisted of 10 or 12 sales agents. He and some of the agents traveled with their spouses. They were all sales professionals. Jose Silva was clearly outclassed! In the morning, everybody met at Rodriguez's hotel room. From there, they take out the inventory they want for the day. They have a carrying device designed to hold up to 10 frames. The frame was made of very inexpensive materials but smartly done to look good to the buyer. Neg still has one of these frames now 55 years later! It probably cost one to two pesos at the time to manufacture. It sold for 45 pesos. The sales commission to the agent was six to eight pesos. Minimum salaries for workers at the time were about eight pesos a day. The average agent would check out seven to eight frames. Rodriguez would make several trips in his 1946 Ford coupe, taking the agents to drop them at the areas he would designate for them. They were not allowed to work outside their designated area. This day Jose (and I, for I am the one who carried the inventory) was the last one to be dropped off and given his territory.

So we were on the street, Rodriguez had shown Jose the four city blocks he had for the day and selected the house where he was going to pitch the product so Jose could hear "the argument." He knocked on the door, and a lady came out. We introduced ourselves, and Rodriguez proceeded to lay the pitch on her. All this time, I was hanging on every word that came out of Rodriguez's mouth. He slickly made the sale, showed Jose how to write it up, collected the down payment, etc. We were set up for the rest of the day. I don't remember how many sales Jose made that day.

By the end of that day, I came to the conclusion that I could do this and begged Rodriguez to give me a chance. He had more reasons to say no than yes. The group consisted of mostly family men, serious people who had earned their place in his group. He conducted evening sessions where agents would talk about the clients of the day. Sometimes an agent would play the role of a client while another would go through his presentation as the rest critiqued.

The basis for the whole exercise revolved around "the argument." It was like a Bible study session with the argument as the Bible. He gave the group an air of professionalism and dignity. Rodriguez made something unexceptional, exceptional. Allowing a raggedy 14-year-old street kid from Nogales into a position equal to the other agents would not have seemed very smart for a guy like Rodriguez. There would surely be complaints from the group about wasting precious territory on such a kid.

Nevertheless, Rodriguez agreed to give me a chance! I don't remember what convinced him. My first day as a salesman, I was in line with the other agents to pick up the frames. I asked for 10. Everybody in the room did a double take! They looked at me like I was too big for my britches!

We go in the field, I get dropped off, I get my territory for the day. By early afternoon, I was back at Rodriguez's room asking for more inventory and more territory. He could not believe it. He said this had never happened before. He gave me more inventory and took me out again. He didn't want to seem too optimistic: it could be just beginner's luck. No chance. From that day forward, I was the top producer. No one came close, even as overall sales increased. I had raised the bar.

The Nogales market was exhausted now. It was time to move on to the next town. It was time for Rodriguez to come and meet Neg and talk to her about giving me permission to go on the road with them. He promised to look after me as if I were his own son. It was not easy for her to let go, but she had faced tougher decisions. At least this one had an upside.

From Nogales, we went to Cananea, then to Agua Prieta and Magdalena, then to neighboring towns and hamlets such as Imuris, San Ignacio, Santa Anna, Benjamin Hill, etc. then over to Caborca and San Luis Rio Colorado and the other small towns as we ended the Sonora tour on the state's western border. From there, we went to Mexicali and began the Baja California tour.

It was 1956 now. With the money I'd been sending Neg, she bought a residential lot in a humble subdivision in the outskirts of town. She and Cundi started to build a one-room house.

Cip was in Guadalajara, but his plans called for him to relocate to Tijuana where he could more easily expedite the process of documentation for relocating to the US. He moved to Tijuana probably by the end of the first quarter.

January of 1956 found the group in Ensenada. We had spent the month of December in Tijuana, where I turned 15. Tio Juan found out I was there and came to visit me. I don't remember much from his visit.

By this time in the tour, I had honed my "craft." I acquired some tools. I wore only dress shoes, pants and shirts. I had two, maybe three ties, including my favorite bow tie. I had at least two sport coats. I kept my hair short, like a military cut, so I could play the "seminarista" card when necessary. I would imply that I was working my way through the seminary to become a priest.

By now my Spanish was impeccable. My enunciation was clean and precise. When I was spinning my version of "the argument," I could see mothers getting impatient to buy whatever it was I was selling. I felt like I had a gift.

In April of 1956, the tour was coming to an end for me. We were in the beautiful city of La Paz, the towns of San Jose del Cabo and Cabo San Lucas, etc. From here the group was going to Guadalajara and then through central and southern Mexico. For me, it had been an adventure, but it was time to go back to Neg and Nogales. From

La Paz, I took a plane to Loreto then across the gulf to Guaymas, then a bus to Nogales.

The one-room home Neg and Cundi were building was now completed enough for them to move in. The clan was no longer in the downtown barrio of El Embarcadero. We now lived in the barrio of El Panteón. Instead of going to Pestalozi school, Juan went to a school by International street. We all lived together: Neg, Cundi, Cundi's mother, Doña Catalina, Doña Josefina (an old lady who stayed with us, but I don't remember why), Raymundo (Cundi's nephew about the same age as Juan who was turned over to the care of Cundi and Neg), Juan and me. I don't know if I am missing anybody else. Suffice to say, there were a lot of us!

After a couple of days in Nogales, I dropped by Sonora Electric to say hi. Jesus Cano asked me to come and work for them. I told him it did not look like he had any openings available. He said that was not a problem, he would make up a position for me. The setup was, he was the owner and manager, next Don Pedro who was the electronics tech, then Saenz who did the deliveries and occasionally helped with in-house sales, then "Luchy" the secretary, and Rascon (this was Jose Silva's replacement). I don't remember what happened to Jose Silva. Rascon was a cowboy type from Arizona who did outside sales strictly on commission. Then there were the *cobradores* (debt collectors): "El Viejito" (I don't remember his name), el "Pachi" (Isidro Aldecoa), el "Fili" (Filiberto Gonzales) and el "Fai" (Rafael Hernandez).

Because 95 percent of the sales are done on credit, these cobradores were the lifeline of the business. Each of these guys had their own "territory" in Nogales. Cano had them select from their accounts the ones that gave them the most problems and turned them over to me. In effect, Cano created a new territory for me that encompassed all their territories. Soon I was repossessing radios, irons, furniture, etc. These things had no value whatsoever, they went straight to the dump, but with a new sheriff in town, the other accounts seemed to pick up the pace. While all this was going on, I baptized Fili's firstborn and Fai's firstborn, so we were now compadres. This was the beginning of a long list of baptisms; everybody and his brother wanted me to be their compadre.

Cip by now was working in the larger "cesspool" city of Tijuana. He had initiated the documentation process to go to the US to work. Henry and Helen Lopez were the sponsors of record. Neg and Cundi had also started working on Neg's documents. As a US citizen, Cundi could bring his wife into the US to join him.

I was having a hell of a good time in Nogales. Nevertheless, Neg and Prieto convinced me to start the documentation process to join them in the US. Beto Reyes would act as my sponsor.

Cano, the owner of the furniture store (everyone had a nickname, his was el chato, because he had a big nose) was a high-profile person in the community. He would later become presidente municipal or mayor. He knew I would be leaving soon and tried to talk me out of it. I don't remember if he made any promises to convince me to stay, but I remember him saying that I would lose any sense of individuality in the US. I would become just another social security number, he warned.

The United States of America Period (Phase 1)

Cip immigrated to the US in March of 1957. Tia Lupe welcomed him to the Reyes household. For the first time in many years, he is now among friendly faces in a loving environment with supportive people all around. It was a totally foreign experience for him! Such conditions and circumstances would eventually make him able to trust people again, at least to a level where the machete scars on the back of his psyche would fade in the distance, maybe even have a fighting chance of some kind of life.

The Reyes children were all on their own now. Nena was married to Henry Lopes; their children were Sylvia, Carolina and Guero (Henry). Lalo was married to Marlene. Their children were Cathy, Eddie, Larry and Esteban. Beto was married to "China" (Virginia). They had Christie and Rena. Lonnie (Jo) was married to Ray Garcia.

They had Tony (Tadzio), Jo and Terri. Lina married Gilbert Ramos, and their children were Gilbert (Pudgee), David and Leo.

Within this geographic area were Tio Juan and his kids. This branch included Sylvia, married to Valentin, Lucy and her husband Paul, Josefina and her husband Richard and, of course, the oldest daughter Dolores and Juan Lopes. At this point in time, they live in Tucson.

The family tree branch of Tia Josefina and Tio Santiago Canales now includes Carmen, Esperanza Juan, Josefina, Miguel, Santiago, Rita, Enrique, Maria and Luis.

The Reyes found Cip a job with a wholesale hardware distributor catering to the aviation industry. Soon, after a couple of promotions, he is a supervisor and buyer. Concurrently with this, after he got familiar with things, he started a janitorial service. I do not know how many employees he had, but now he had a full-time job, plus he had his own humble little business, including equipment to operate the business, his own place and a late model car.

Neg's documents are ready now, and she and Cundi move to Tucson on September 9, 1957. They move into a small rental unit Cundi's sister Susana and husband Gilbert have. I stay behind in Nogales, as my papers are about to be ready at any moment.

So is late Friday afternoon in 1957 in downtown Nogales. Downtown begins at the border and stretches south, the main part consisting of one street a mile or so long. It's lined with bars, curio shops, restaurants, other supplementary business, banks, beauty shops, money exchange houses, etc. Traffic is always terrible, however, beginning Friday and through the weekend, is a loud, nightmarish bumper-to-bumper mess. The heart of downtown is the intersection of Calle Campillo and Avenida Obregón. On the northeast corner is El Regis. This is an upscale (such as upscale is) bar and pool hall. On the northwest corner is La Frontera. This is a bar, one of several that claim to be a "ladies bar." The fact that these bars had big signs proclaiming to be ladies bars is an illustration of the clash of two cultures. A fender bender of the two collective realities. Up until now, and outside of this little world of Nogales, no one could ever imagine seeing a female specimen of the human species in a bar, unless of course you were in the red-light district. On the southeast corner is the Hotel Fray Marcos De Niza. As far as I am concerned, at the time this is for me one of the seven wonders of the world. Can you believe it? Is a whopping nine or 10 stories high!

I don't remember what's on the southwest corner. Right next to it, though, facing Calle Campillo, is another bar and pool hall called El Concordia. On this side of Calle Campillo in front of this bar, parking is reserved for taxi cabs. This bar is of special interest to me and my friends, because it has the reputation that the best pool *carambola* players of the region hang here. My friends and I are hooked on carambola. It was not unusual for us to pull all-nighters either playing or watching the masters play.

So where was I? Oh yeah, I am 16 years old. I am in the cesspool town of Nogales, Sonora. It is late Friday afternoon, and my friends and I are hanging out at the southeast corner of Campillo and Obregón. I'm probably wearing one of my three tailored suits. They were made just the way I like them: the pants not hemmed, not high or low rise, the belt loops about three fourths of an inch high, just enough for a thin belt. Actually, it was not even a belt, because the pants are made to fit me perfectly; there's no need for a belt, just the promise of a belt. There is a slight break in the crease, just after it scarcely touches the laced part of my shoe. The lapels of the jacket are long and not wide, but slim, coming down to a single button. One of the suits is gray; the other is slightly darker than light brown, and the third is a grayish blue. I'm probably wearing the gray.

There's wall-to-wall people, traffic noise, vendors' noise, music emanating from different bars… The environment is abuzz with energy. So my friends and I are having a good time, just hanging there and watching the girls of all ages, shapes and colors go by (this scenario and moment, that follows, remains etched in my memory even after all these years). Then this beautiful, slick, black, latest model, hardtop Bel Air with all the bells and whistles pulls over from traffic in front of me. The door opens, and the people inside motion me to get in. At a heartbeat, without wasting any time, I get in! I had never seen these people before! Driving the car is Ray, Lonnie's husband. Lonnie is riding shotgun. In the back seat are my later to be compadres Gilbert and Lina Ramos and Cip. Over the years, my compa Gilbert has described on several occasions what was going on in the car at this very moment. They had just crossed the border into Mexico and into the middle of the heavy downtown traffic and the crowded sidewalks. They were discussing how in the world they were going to manage to find me. Right about this time, he tells me, he looks out the window and even though he had never seen me before, he knows it's me. He yells, "There he is!" And sure enough, there I was. I did not know they were coming; it was one hell of a surprise! They had taken the weekend off to drive from Van Nuys to Nogales, with Cip as their guide, to meet their cousin from the old country.

By the end of this same month, my papers are ready as well, and I follow shortly thereafter to join Neg and Cundi in Tucson.

Part Two

What Kind of Game Is This? Can Anyone Play?

The ripples made by raindrops falling on puddles made the light of street lamps seem to dance up and down, an inadvertent mockery of the tremendous grief that Emilio was feeling. The moon was just hanging there, as his tears went rolling down his cheeks. It was as if the rain were... wait, wait, wait a moment, *Wero*, never mind this. Let's get back to the business at hand.

Earlier I warned you I would be telling you more about my pedestrian interest in things like reality, etc. I know it sounds ambitious or pretentious or both, but what the heck, you read this far, you might as well keep reading.

Here is a disclaimer: As you indulge me and my comments about reality, time, space, etc., bear in mind that my intent is not to get in the same league with the proposals made by movies like *The Matrix*, *Inception*, etc. My viewpoint is "sidewalk level"—not in conflict nor in common with them.

Communication has always fascinated me because it plays a major role in circulating reality.

Ideas and concepts are usually easier to communicate than feelings and emotions. We are governed by feelings and emotions, so one would think it would be the other way around. It is a design feature of nature that is cleverly analyzed in the dialogues between Star Trek characters Bones, Captain Kirk and Mr Spock.

I am fascinated by what this design feature in us does to the mechanics of everyday life. This fascination has to do with how it is that we have built-in mechanisms designed to impede our capacity to communicate at the same time that our capacity to be happy in life is directly dependent on our capacity to communicate.

So why did Mother Nature see fit to build this feature into the motor that generates the volition required to communicate?

On second thought, perhaps it is too soon still to ask why. We can look at the pitfalls of "why" later. For now, let's talk about the nuts and bolts of this design feature.

The character in each of the four basic elements (air, "oith", fire and water) is extended to the four basic races: white, red, black and yellow, and then to the personality quadrant of driver, analytical, amiable and expressive. The characteristics that make the four elements different from each other are also embedded in each race at their most basic level. These differences are also extended to their languages and their mode of expression. For example, English or German could be said to be mechanical, or the driver in the personality quadrant (logical Spock), as opposed to romantic Spanish or French (expressive Bones).

These characteristics are innately embedded in the collective minds of their respective races and, therefore, extended to their respective collective personalities or cultural identities. So all of these components are in place before an individual begins to learn to articulate words. Then environment is left with the task of teaching individuals how to communicate.

On one end, the environment has a poor bastard suicide bomber convinced he wants to kill himself. On the other end, environment has a wife in Green Valley, Arizona, convinced her husband is a bastard because he forgot their anniversary. She is not aware that hospitals worldwide implant microchips in all newborn male babies that make them recoil from cuddling and forget anniversaries. For decades, he has tried different ways to explain to her the presence of this chip. She has heard his explanations; however, she has a chip that distinguishes between hearing and listening, allowing the former while blocking the latter.

If we agree that feelings/emotions govern our thoughts and thoughts manufacture our reality and our words are one of the first lines of distribution of that reality, we would be easily discouraged by that setup. At the same time, however, we may be encouraged by the fact that we start from a level playing field: if you were born, you have it.

This difficulty was shared by great prophets, poets and teachers alike, including Jesus, Moses, Krishna, Pythagoras, etc. Their challenge was more extreme because they had to work with existing communications practices and symbols to explain new concepts. It remains a point of debate how successful they were in getting their point across. Jesus's method is probably the most widely known. One of his tools for communicating is the parable. What we know of his life is all metaphorical since most theologians agree we know very little or nothing of his historical life. From conception to ascension, He is a walking, talking, breathing parable of what our relative life is in this plane. To this day in communication seminars the world over, they advise you to start with a story if you want people to remember the message—just like Jesus did.

Nature made it difficult for us to communicate with one another, but that is not all. To make it even more interesting, we constantly forget that in time and space, things are never the same. Today seems the same as yesterday, and tomorrow will seem the same as today. But it is different in time and so many other ways. The moment it takes me right now to press this key on the keyboard is already different from the one before and different from the next. Everything is in constant movement and therefore in constant change.

The movement of the planets (the Incas referred to Jupiter as Father Time), the wobble of the oith, the thoughts of the individuals therein, etc., make each day in our current recorded time different from any other day in our current recorded history.

Time and space in our third dimensional world are the professional agitators under reality's payroll. The job for time and space is to veil reality. So, if in time and space things are never the same, then in reality things are never what you think they are.

That these mechanisms exist in nature reminds me of the simulator program *Kobayashi Maru*. As you know, this is a test for cadets at the Federation of Planets Academy.

This test is designed with a "no win" scenario where whoever takes it will fail.

Perhaps now is an appropriate time to introduce another disclaimer. Please note that if I drop words like *time, space, art,* etc. is not that I know what they are or understand them. That deer in the middle of the road in the middle of the night has not even a remote idea that the light coming at him is from a semi-trailer truck. For that moment, the light just fascinates and freezes him.

EN. Hey, Briones!
ME. Hey, Emilio Noir! Where the hell you been? You bean, why do you interrupt me now?

EN. 'Cause you are about to make me barf with all this time and space crap!

Me. Now is not a good time for you to surface. You gonna make lose my train of thought!

EN. Train of thought? Now I'm really gonna barf!

Me. Shut the fuck up, Emilio. Control yourself. I'll get back to you later.

That bastard! After all these years, I still never know when he just wants to bug me or wants to keep me honest or wants to enable me by telling me the things I want to hear, bastard!

Where was I? Oh yeah, there are some feelings, emotions, and traits—some of which makes us do things that can't be explained with words alone. We have known of this impediment all along, as evidenced by the emergence of mythological figures, fairy tales, theater, etc. The need to have these tools of expression was obvious even that far back. So now, in addition to tools like poetry, music, and literature to help explain feeling and emotions, we have movies and television.

Movies are excellent modern-day parables. We are extremely lucky to have this medium available for expression, even in spite of the "squeaky clean," antiseptically silly, "white bread" life situations portrayed in the Doris Day / Rock Hudson movies. Television has potential too, in spite of the harmful presence of characters like Dr. Phil, Oprah Winfrey and others who have the compassion of paper cups.

Emilio. Doris Day, Rock Hudson? Who tha fuck are they?

Me. Shut da fuck up! And stop interrupting!

That pain in the behind Emilio! He knows it's relevant to mention Rock Hudson and Doris Day because the characters they portray in their movies helped plant the seeds of depression, prevalent today, which are fed and preserved by the self-serving, uncompassionate Oprahs and Phils.

Okay, back to the magic of communication. These tools (poetry, music, etc.) have an intangible component: their ability to invoke feelings and emotions. I do not know what it is, but I know it is there because of how it plays with our lives—kind of an "unreasonable reason." *Unreasonable* because it cannot be explained reasonably, and *reason* because it explains a lot of the illogical things we do in life. You would think this thing would have a name. Maybe this is one of those few things that cannot be named (at least not in our limited understanding).

So, we have in our brain all this equipment, mechanisms, conditionings, etc., that together make up the industry or the infrastructure that is in the business of collating the information communicated to us and transforming it into reality, as rendered from our particular perspective.

EN. Whaaaatt?
ME. Fuck off, Emilio!

Bastard! Not now!

Western thought is one of the main suppliers of the material used in the conditionings forming our reality. Let's check this vendor's résumé as we would any other vendor soliciting our business.

Western thought (this is usually when Emilio Noir tells me to climb down, from up my own ass) took a more noticeable direction (probably sometime in the seventeenth century) when science (reason) began to compete with religion, the arts, etc. (unreason, magic) for dominion over Western civilization's psyche.

After the Second World War, science was secured as the undisputed leader (magic lost the competition). This looked justifiably so; after all, science had made and continues to make incredible accomplishments. So the trend was that anything that could not be scientifically explained lost credibility. Therefore, magic, religion and spirituality lost their place in the consciousness of individuals. At about the same time, Eastern thought (a competing supplier to reality) went the other way. In India, for example, that part of the world not being in the "loop" of the age of enlightenment, they were left with a spirituality without science, thereby not recognizing the need for social service and getting all screwed up in their relationship with their physicality. The sad social status of women in these parts of the world must surely be related to this. One might say they got top heavy with religion to the point where it was not religion anymore. It became something else. Therefore, they got as lost as the West but at opposite ends of the collective reality spectrum.

Scientific accomplishments, for the purpose of this argument, are valid and have their place and contributions to make to our consciousness and reality, except that science without spirituality is not complete. In the movie *Nacho Libre,* in one of many incredibly funny moments, Nacho, being a priest, is trying to convert his partner, Eskeleto, to religion. Since they are at that moment about to get a terrible beating at the hands of their opponents, he asks Eskeleto, "Don't you believe in God?" He answers, "No, I don't. I choose science." It is his way of telling Nacho there is no hope for them.

The post-Second World War reality prompted all of us to choose science; it was the thing to do at the time. According to "new age" commentators from the 1980s and 90s, science without spirituality is playing a major role in producing the current "fragmented reality."

The trend today, though, according to them, appears to be that we in the West have begun to realize that our reality is missing the contributions from the "unreason" part of the arts and mythology. This, though, sounds to me like mostly wishful thinking from people who do not wish you well.

Some of these commentators agree that pioneering this trend were Latin American literary artists Carlos Fuentes and Gabriel Garcia Marquez. Based on this, I plan to continue to use Western thought as one of my suppliers and vendors of materials for the construction of reality.

In order to get materials from other suppliers or to cut out the middleman and produce our own materials in house for the production of our own reality (whatever that may be), I tell the Picard (this is what I call my grandson Sergio) that anything any individual does should have at least a component of ethics, a component of service and a component of compassion. Together with these, according to

Mr. Magorium (from the Dustin Hoffman movie), each day and each task should be approached with determination, bravery and joy (reference is hereby made as to how everything is in groups of three).

Along those lines, everything an individual, a community, or a nation does in life has three aspects or three values or a three-pronged impact. Any single thought, word or action has this three-pronged impact.

They are the public, the personal, and the intimate. The terms *public, personal,* and *intimate* are used here simply to be able to somehow tell them apart. In Christianity, the equivalent is the Father, the Son, and the Holy Spirit. Or in Eastern philosophy, the gross physical body, the astral body, seat of man's mental and emotional nature, and the ethereal body. Or put another way, the reptilian brain, the limbic brain and the neocortex.

In Jesus's ministry (I should really introduce another disclaimer here), in the public aspect, is the message he disseminated to the masses; the sermon on the mount represents a résumé of this message. An individual's relationship with work or school and with his teachers, with his community or his government belong by nature in the public aspect of his life. When this type of relationship becomes personal, it creates an imbalance, not unlike the imbalance Barbra Streisand's character had in the movie *The Way We Were.*

So whether public, personal or intimate, each brings with it the three aspects in their own right. Then each of those brings three of their own, and so on and so forth. From three months from inception, the individual begins to record everything that occurs in its periphery; everything there in recorded carries this three-pronged impact, and thus, the fabric of reality is weaved.

The personal aspect includes things that have to do with the immediate family and friends (including offspring). Jesus's personal part of his ministry includes the message he communicated to the apostles, one quite different from the public one. Here, the message is more specific. The goals more defined; the how-to is clear, or at least clearly explained by Jesus. I am convinced this is one the apostles had a big problem conceptualizing, to the frustration of Jesus. So here, even though the interchange is clearly personal, the impact on the recipient will carry a resultant public, personal and intimate effect. I speculate organized religion is deficient at resonating at the personal level. Let me explain what I mean by *resonating*. To do this, I have to quote from Scripture.

EMILIO NOIR. Chuy, you uppity peasant! You are the last person on Oith that should be quoting Scripture! You heathen! You, you should be struck by lightning, burned in brimstone, etc., Better yet, I'll tell your cousin Lina Ramos, she'll fix your little red wagon. She'll fix it with a sledgehammer!

Me: I'm warning you, Emilio! Shut up. Remember, I used to be a plumber. I can turn your water off!

Okay, back to Scripture.

The angel Gabriel and Mary at the Annunciation.

"The Holy Spirit will come upon you, and the power of the Most High will overshadow you; therefore the child to be born from you will be holy; he will be called the Son of God" (Luke 1:35 KJV).

You live next door to Mary and Joseph and your neighbor from down the street, Mr. Organized Religion (I am okay with organized religion, I'll explain why later) comes to tell you all about Gabriel's visit. Everybody is naturally moved and happy; they are such nice and kind neighbors. But you are happy for them, not for yourself; after all, this has no direct impact on you, that you are aware of. Organized religion today is not organized to transport (communicate) into your mind and heart the feeling of knowing that this verse is describing a condition of divinity available to any would-be mothers and fathers in the world.

EMILIO NOIR. All this sounds pretty patronizing to me.

ME. Dammed, you again? You might be right. I just want to illustrate the pitfalls of communicating by quoting Scripture. Unless you transmit the intended feeling, the verse will be little more than just another concept or just another idea, more words, mostly wasted saliva.

Just to further burn your ass, Emilio, here is another example (I only know it in Spanish).

> Dios te salve Maria
> Llena eres de Gracia
> El Señor es contigo
> Bendita tu eres
> Entre todas las mujeres
> Bendito es el fruto
> De tu vientre Jesus.

I love this greeting. In one of its aspects, it describes a condition of grace available by birthright to all the women of the world. For the communication to be complete, these two examples have to resonate in the individual in all three aspects. It probably never reaches the reptilian brain.

Let's see, where was I? Oh yeah, the intimate aspect. In the intimate is where an individual can find genuine rest, where his humanity can gain strength. Here too, like in the other two, the results will have the usual threefold impact. Jesus's intimate (metaphorical) life is the one he shared with Mary of Bethany and Mary Magdalene (modern biblical scholars believe they are one and the same). The intimate aspect of our lives is deficient; any two individuals sharing the same roof need incredible amounts of mutual support and constant mutual nurturing. Single parents' challenges are beyond my capacity to describe.

Deficiencies that resonate more at the intimate level often result in actions lacking compassion, redirecting the focus from the things that matter at that one specific moment in that specific space. One extreme is the poor moron (for the sake of making a point, there is no compassion in this statement) suicide bomber. His reality is a product of an environment that does not produce the opportunity or is not conducive to the existence of an intimate aspect that would be nurturing or supportive. It does not matter how though the living conditions or how great the injustices, an individual can overcome anything if his intimate life is in balance. This balance often produces a purpose positive to his life. As long as women have the same social status as dirt in his environment, the odds are against this poor bastard. The equivalent of this guy in the United States are the Trump supporters.

So in the case of the wife in Green Valley, before she can address the fact that he forgot their anniversary (the anniversary thing is used here to illustrate a mindset), even though her environment is constantly telling her this is a big deal, she has to focus first on what really matters at that specific moment, at that specific space. Chastising the poor bastard can never be supportive or nurturing and will only result in, at best, feelings of guilt. In an environment where most everything we do is driven by the feeling of fear, she is now adding a feeling of guilt. Her environment is also making her want to compete with the poor bastard. If she only knew she doesn't have to compete! Contrary to her conditioning, she does not realize that,

> Ilena eres de Gracia
> El Señor es contigo
> Bendita tu eres

If she could only be aware that *this is not a game about being right or wrong.* You can be right and still lose. When one loses, everybody loses.

"And I saw the holy city, new Jerusalem, arrayed as a bride for her husband" (Revelations 21:2).

I'm beyond the point of return with Emilio Noir. My problem now is with my cousin/sister Lina Ramos. She is probably by now collecting signatures to have me struck by lightning! I'll just keep going…

Cosmic energy is manifested on Oith, as male and female energy; anybody drawing a breath has both of them. However, she (the Green Valley wife) is the keeper of the female energy, the vessel, the Holy Grail. She is the archetype, the Isis, the Magdalene, the Guadalupe.

She is more than a wife. She is a priestess on earth to—in communion with her husband, in the intimacy of their inner sanctum, in their holy of holies—keep the order of the universe intact.

Here, in their moments of communion, she, using her nurturing nature (a virtue of her female energy) and her sacred rituals, soothes his nature. This is the only place where he can afford true rest. This is the only place where he can gain strength. From here, he can go into the world and overcome any adversity, storm the castle. But most important of all (are you paying attention, EN?), from here he can sustain and continue the constant struggle to reconcile the contradictions in his nature.

From here, they together go through their Kobayashi Maru. Not unlike Faust in Goethe's poem, where his ass is grass because he has to make good in his deal with the devil and pay with his soul. But thanks to the intervention of the Feminine Principle, he is redeemed.

EMILIO NOIR. Dammed, chuy! What ta fudge! That's deep!
ME. How the fudge would you know? You don't even know how to keep your fly zipped! Enough already with the interruptions!

MARC BRIONES

So where was I. Oh yeah, reason.

After Marc's accident (my son, 11-24-1984/ 02-10-2003), the small communities of Sahuarita and Green Valley rallied in support of the families of the victims. The accident had a high profile in the community. At Marc's services, just by the count in the sign in book, there were more than 800 people, and those were only the ones who bothered to sign. The march in front of the coffin went on non-stop. The parking lot of the funeral home was packed with people, traffic jams, etc.

roadside grave marker
Sahuarita, Arizona

There was a letter to the editor of the *Arizona Daily Star* that I believe is a good representation of the reason side of our community. The letter's author supported what some in the community called the negative reporting of the accident by the media and the authorities and was complaining about the effort of support from the community to the families of the victims. Saying that the support given was a bad example, that the actions that led to the accident should be condemned.

Those individuals, dressed in garments made of prudency and caution, would say that the guy who wrote the letter is right, that reason is on his side. Perhaps reason is on his side. At that moment, though, if I had to say anything, I would say, fuck reason.

There are times when nations, communities and individuals need to put reason below the top of the list. I can tell you that going through this has to be worse than death itself. I can say this because (reality being what it is or is not) I am convinced that at least once in my life, I faced death. The prospect of dying at that moment was nothing compared to the physical pain, the inexplicable pain in the chest, something else (I do not know what it was) manifested by sudden weaknesses in the knees and a profound and heavy sense of sadness with uncontrollable bursts of tears. So Ida, me, Kevin, the individual families and the community were in crisis.

At times like these, science can do nothing for me. What we needed were nurturing, compassion, support, healing... There would be time for reason later.

Up until the time of Juan's passing (May 22, 1998), I had not understood why organized religion exists. My environment and my conditioning did not fully justify their existence. For my father, organized religion and the mainstream medical profession were two institutions to be avoided. Therefore, at the time of his passing, there were no services of any kind. His corpse went straight from the hospital to cremation. I now know, by this action, I was very wrong.

During the pain and sadness of Juan's passing, I found myself grateful to the Catholic organization. I was grateful the organization was there for us. The family had a place to go. I was grateful for the sense of community it affords. In terms of how this sense of community provides a type of opportunity for some type of release. Probably all of this is common knowledge for everyone, but for me, it is totally new. There is something else though, during the services at the church, etc., and in light of what all this (Catholicism) represents, I got the sense of a mixture of validation, pride, belonging and a bunch of other like feelings. I am sure at the audience there was a cross section of different denominations other than Catholic. There might have been some in the audience with some matter of fact or moralizing type of criticism for the Catholic institution. I believe it must be painful when one or a loved one gets hurt by some of these institutions. Just like my father must have been hurt by these institutions (religion, medical profession) to the point that he never forgave them. However, at that moment and at other moments in my life thereafter, the Catholic institution provided an opportunity or served as one of several conduits for grief releasing. Not that anyone is asking or listening, but in the name of Neg, Juan, Cip and myself, I want to hear myself say that we are Catholics, loyal to it, and at times of deep sorrow, its mysticism suits me fine.

Juan's death in the middle of the grieving, in the middle of the helplessness in the face of tragedy, brought on a preview to and was a primer to a pain and sadness that was soon to come.

So where was I? I don't know, I forget with all this mixture of subjects.

AUTHOS, A NOSTRO
NOXIO, BAY, GLOY
APEN
AGIA, AGIOS, ISHIROS
AUTHOS
KYRIE ELEISON, KYRIE

EN. Damm, chuy, this is too serious!

ME. Ball up, you pussy! Why do you keep interrupting?

EN. It seems you are not clear about what you are trying to say. And now is even more confusing with these words in Latin.

ME. What I want to say, I want to say it in a way that does not sound like I'm preaching, or that I'm full of myself.

EN. But you are full of yourself!

ME. I know, but this is not about that. I could say that in a world where drugs are prescribed to combat depression, we are a family that when in the face of great emotional distress, we never fell prey to depression. I could say that, but it's not about that, it's about more than that. I trust that if this gets read, someone can figure it out.

EN. What about these words in Latin thing?
ME. Yeah, you are right, I should explain that.

Those are lyrics from an album by Patrick Bernhart named Solaris Universalis. I trust, as you read on, you'll agree it is appropriate to include them as one of the tools we found in our defense.

Life happened to the Sonoran Briones brothers and sister—Cip, Juan, me and Neg—like it happens to everyone. We grew up and went through life together. We have the scars to prove it.

However, we seek to wear our scars with dignity and pride, void of bitterness or gloom or depression. At the time of Marc's tragedy, I experienced an overwhelming sadness. Listening to this music provided for a much-needed healing to take place, not that you ever heal from these things. This music reached a much deeper level in the core of my being, helping nurture my bruised self.

The efforts to provide comfort and support from family, friends and community in this time of need were very helpful and given unconditionally. However, the soothing effect of the music came from a different realm, a different plane void of logic.

Regarding support from friends, two of many come to mind. A business associate at the time, Carl Bosse, set up an appointment for Ida and me with a grief counselor. Ida declined, but I went as a courtesy to Carl. Early in the session, she said, "You are probably wondering why all of this happened." Up until that moment, the "why" had never surfaced in my mind. I explained to her that asking why now was not productive in terms of helping me with my grief. It turned out that something traumatic had happened in her life as well. By the end of the session, I was counseling her.

Another show of support comes to mind. It had been two days since the accident. I had not been able to sleep. I had a lot of restless, nervous energy. I needed to rest and sleep. I needed to be semi-functioning for Ida and Kevin. It was about mid-morning, and I called my friend and handball buddy Eric Healy. "Hey, Eric where are you?"

"In my office." His office being in downtown Tucson.

"Hey, you bastard, how about some handball?"

"Just name the time and place!"

Within half an hour, we were playing at the Downtown Y. There was no "I'm doing this" or the other or "I have this appointment" or the other. He dropped whatever he was doing at the time to go play. As always, he kicked my ass with no mercy. During play, there was no mention, whatsoever, of the accident, or "How you doing?" or anything related. There was no need to say anything.

EN. Thank you for explaining, I'm beginning to see how you are struggling to bring out what you want to say. I feel I need to validate you so you can relax a little bit. For one thing, you had to give some type of background on the art of communicating—especially the point that it is in everyone's nature to be limited in our capacity to communicate. All of the other commentaries about the other subjects are all connected with the nature of communication. You feel it's important to comment on these subjects, at the risk of confusion. You trust there will be a better chance that if anyone reads this, it will not sound like a worn-out cliché and they'll realize the stuff in between the lines.

It is clear to me now that you are doing this because you want to give your family something. Since you don't have money—and even if you had it—you would want to give them something of value.

So I believe you should repeat what you already said here, but in a different way. Also tell us more about the Sonoran Collective. By the way, so you know, your cousin/sister Lina Ramos is okay with you quoting from Scripture.

ME. Thank you, it is good for me to hear you say all that.

So growing up in the old country, from time to time, I would hear the saying, "God does not help those that don't help themselves." Much later in life, I heard it again in one the movie versions of the myth / fairy tale *Beowulf.*

I don't know where the saying originated, but many believe it to be Christian. Along that vein, and often missed, ignored, denied, not read between the lines, never taught anywhere, etc., is where in Christianity during confession you are absolved of your sins. So here it is, you heard it here first. *God will not forgive those who do not forgive themselves first.*

I cannot overstate how important this is. To Jesus's frustration, the apostles never understood this. Standing between Jesus and the apostles on this teaching was the Sanhedrin, the Law of Moses, the fiddler on the roof (ha ha), etc. Freud never even came close to realizing how critical this is. Avant-garde Carl Jung was not successful in communicating it to any degree of consequence.

One thing is to read this and get some concept of what it means. The issue is, however, is how does one forgive oneself? It is worse than trying to draw a perfect circle. Some claim that one can't even imagine a perfect circle, much less draw one. I have come to believe, probably others too, that you have to build in place the structure that will bring you to where you will be able to forgive yourself.

Juan Manuel Coss
6/30/1947–5/22/1998

May 23, 1998. Last Sunday morning when I came in for coffee (as I used to do on a regular basis), we talked a little, maybe he had some kind of a presage. We touched briefly on the challenges our family had been facing lately. We took solace in the thought that such periods are surely followed by periods of great peace. He mentioned how during these phases of challenge how easy it is to start asking questions like "why me" and the like. He likened this to "the futile attempt to understand Creation." We agreed this must be avoided.

He brought up the subject of his job. He worked for Child Protective Services. He often had opportunities to go work someplace else for better money and better work environment. CPS was an agency plagued with (probably still is) unsurmountable problems, bigger than the agency itself. The agency did not have the most important component needed to fulfill its only mission. It did not have compassion. It was (pardon the comparison) like a concrete ready-mix plant not having cement.

Juan had an abundant, unending supply of compassion. Maybe the by-product of his early life in Mexico. Maybe it was the byproduct of being at the receiving end of the unjust built-in mechanisms in the public school system that deflate any ambitions any minority student might be crazy enough to have. Although by this time some had broken the barrier and gone on to get a college education, they were mostly third or second generation. Who spoke the language, sons or daughters of veterans returning from the Second World War with some kind of understanding or compass about navigating a system decked against them? Juan, against all odds, including having to learn a second language, learning to fit in, being that getting good grades is so political, graduated with a bachelor's degree from the University of Arizona. He had the ambition and started to work on a master's degree. However, the support systems available to him for this undertaking were not what they needed to be.

Or maybe he got his compassion from his mother, Neg, a manifestation of compassion herself.

He helped the staff and case workers under him at every opportunity, beyond what would be reasonably expected. He was sensitive to what was going on in their personal lives. He would counsel them on stress management, etc., to help them so they would manage to maintain a measure of compassion serving the "clients" of the agency, among other things. These clients were kids that were in the middle of and victims of some major family crisis, most of them already condemned to a life of violence, drugs, etc. Despite the agency's incredible shortcomings, his commitment to service took precedence over whatever material rewards he could have surely found someplace else.

We covered all this and more, like how he loved to travel, his trips to Europe, Africa and South America, how he was fascinated by France, etc.

In what turned out to be our last conversation, he gave me a piece of paper with these words (I'm not sure who wrote it):

> As dreary as the path might seem to those
> who view it from afar, it has tender lights and
> restful shades that no other walk in life can give.
> Rejoice! These are your wilderness days and
> surely and safely you are being led.

He was probably preparing me for things on the horizon. A few months earlier, he introduced me to Bernhardt's Solaris Universalis. When he fell ill, the family and those close to him from work were with him in his last days, demonstrating great love and affection.

> Juan Coss, Juan Coss
> We feel such a loss,
> You left us too soon to sail past the Moon
> and journey beyond bright solar bombs,
> To explore all worlds, both inner and outer,
> You are a believer, not a doubter;
> Still, you have this thirst to see personally
> the wonders of yore and visions undead…
> Oh look up ahead, there's a note on your bed
> It says, *"I'm out until late, if you like you can wait.*
> *When I return I'll have much to say*
> *and together we'll laugh on this marvelous day"*

From "On the Trail" by G.J.Ramos

Cipriano Briones
July 5,1935–February 17, 2008
You shall know them by their works. (Mathew 7:16)

He worked every day of his life down to the last moments. In his last days in the hospital, he was mostly unconscious. At one time when he regained consciousness, Angelica was by his bedside. He recognized her and told her to call Rogelio to remind him it is time to do pest control. To most people, it would be difficult to understand this type of dedication to work. But to those who know us (FYI, we, us, our, ours means Juan, Cip, Neg and me) and are familiar with our background, it's not surprising. We are one of those families that, beyond being thankful for all the blessings bestowed on us, are thankful as well for the fortune of living in this country.

While acknowledging our blessed lives and the positive aspects of the mechanics of life in our society, we also acknowledged the negatives—from one end of the spectrum, such as the homeless community in the richest country in the world, to the other end, such as the problems of the upper middle class, and everything in between.

We did this not to pick on anyone, but just to serve as an illustration: for example, how did the homeless get to be homeless? Surely not all were born homeless. The homeless come from all walks of life, not exclusive to one class or profession. There are examples of personal and collective failure in all professions, such as the collective failure of the architectural profession, as it relates to residential architecture. They have given in under pressure from housing developers bent on creating communities void of any sense of individuality or personality. In terms of sociability, this is important because how an individual relates to the spaces in which he dwells is directly related to how well he is going to function in his world.

Of the professions and arts, however, the ultimate disservice in our society comes from the medical profession. I would like to believe (naively) that all the medical doctors and the specialties therein, when deciding to become health professionals, they had the genuine ambition to heal people. But something happened along the way. Society in general and their system to practice medicine, in particular, became geared toward making them fail from the get-go. They give in too easily to all the pressures in society and the system. They wrongly believe they must have big houses, decadent lifestyles, country club memberships, expensive toys, etc., without the time to spend with their patients to help really get to the root of their problems, not just treat the symptoms. If they choose to stay on this path, as most do, the system will render them void of compassion. They become another concrete ready-mix plant, with all the equipment at their disposal, but without any cement in inventory.

My point in all this is that all these professionals, with all the education and extensive training, appear not to see this? What is the Sonoran Briones collective to do? They already have their hands full adjusting to a different culture, navigating a new language, etc.

There are many things we don't know, but we do know we have many things to be thankful for. We also know that not all life's pitfalls are recognizable. After all, trained professionals, intellectually superior to us, don't seem to see them (intellectually superior does not mean smarter or wiser). What do we do? Do we do like most? Do we value the same things and take a chance that someday we'll wake up homeless or worse, incapable of compassion? How are we going to be different?

Every day for many years up until the end of his life, Cipriano would fly the flag. He had to buy several flags per year, as they deteriorated fast. This served him as one mechanism to remind himself to be thankful for all the blessings upon our family.

What else do we sense? Whatever we do, the way we are to do it has to be simple. It also has to be done right, but it has to be done right for the sake of doing it right, nothing else. This probably gave us a sense of ethics, even though I never heard this term until much later in life. Of course, it's not like if we had meetings to strategize or plan to do things this way or the other. We all silently knew all of this.

Cipriano brought the no-nonsense component into our collective. From somewhere, he was given the nasty chore of keeping the rest of us grounded. He saved my ass, economically several times. He also saved me from myself several times.

After his divorce, his lifestyle turned little by little more ascetic and austere. His every action had his own brand of silent humility and dedication to service. Everything he did benefited the collective or someone near to him.

During the late 1970s to the early 1990s, the city of Tucson had a Neighborhood Redevelopment Program. Under this program, the city would go into certain neighborhoods and take inventory of the homes in disrepair. For the homes that were beyond repair, they would give the homeowner the opportunity to have a new home built at no cost to them. There were several builders participating in the program. The homeowner would solicit bids from the builders in the program. Under the city's supervision, the homeowner would select the low bidder. The bids were very competitive.

During this period, there was a crisis in the construction industry. First, there was the Jimmy Carter period of astronomical interest rates, then the historic savings and loan debacle. Everybody and his brother were going bankrupt, from the banking institutions to the appraisers and everyone in between. It was a windfall for bankruptcy lawyers. That made the bids under this program highly competitive. There were too many dogs after the same bone. In spite of this, there was a big turnover of builders participating in this program. The difference in dollar amounts between the bids was very small, but the difference in the product was often substantial.

Del Bac was consistently getting more than the lion's share of the jobs. Builders would come into the program hungry to make a dollar. After a house or two, they would conclude they could not

74

provide the same level of quality or service as Del Bac did. Not only was Cipriano building a home of superior workmanship, afforded by virtue of our simple lifestyle and simple needs, he was firstly doing a good job for the sake of doing a good job, nothing else.

His service went beyond the call of duty. Most of the home-owners were elderly people. For some of them, their support systems were not nearby, so he would take time to check on them regularly. For some, he would even do their grocery shopping or bring them toiletries, etc. I remember a lady whom he would help run her household: pay her utilities and other bills, help with correspondence, etc. By comparison, other builders were never seen again once the house was complete.

A Starchild once I did know,
Dropped in my dream as Greta Garbo.
Translucent and slim, he said, "I am him,"
"Your friend from long time ago"

Yes it was he but was not,
For his features were off,
Yet his essence was decidedly so.
With eyes wide apart
And strange pupils like darts,
He had entered my path ahead
Calmly he turned and gently he said:
"Why carry your load some cranky old toad?
You're bigger than that, you know it's a fact
So pull your head out and give way a shout
You're as free as you want to be!"

With that he was gone beyond the beyond
And left me behind, his straight words on my mind;

Recalling the depth of his speech,
I now wonder when he'll return again
And offer sweet gems that beseech.

Beautiful Creep, Our Dear Cipriano

The echoes of your sing along laughter
resound in our saddened minds
And the joyous burst of your unbridled reverie,
which announced mirth and whimsy,
has been temporarily muted.

We shall see you no more for now, but despair not;
For our irreverent discourses
shall soon manifest
in another place and time
(when the will for the Supreme
has updated our accounts)
and we embark on yet another journey
to herald the dawning of Light and Love.

From "On the Trail" by G.J.Ramos

From time to time, he would have problems with the city administrators in charge of this program. They kept reminding him that he was building government housing, and his homes looked too good for that. To this day, one can drive through the neighborhoods and see the testament to this.

I remember one time when Jesus Manuel, one of the building inspectors under this program, came to tell me that Cipriano had given notice to his boss that he was dropping out of the program. He came to ask me to convince Cipriano not to do it. Of course, I asked him why he wanted me to do that. His job would be a little harder, he said, because he could not control the drop in quality that was sure to happen with Del Bac out of the program.

For us in general, and for Cipriano in particular, work and service, simple values, simple needs were a good fit and our way of being different. These principles kept us on the straight and narrow. Life happens in our world, same as others, except that the innate quality of enthusiasm in every human in the Briones' collective is not under as many layers of false values. In us, what matters is closer to the surface. Those of us near Cip are forever grateful for his impact on the collective. We all miss his brand of devotion.

Though I never said to your face, Cip, I love you.

Josefina Briones Coss
April 8,1933–September 4, 2015

I remember my sister as someone who had unconditional love for anyone she met. No one was excluded from her kindness. There is abnegation in her brand of kindness, it always came with acts of service or sacrifice, even at a very early age in rural Mexico. She was 10 years old when our mother died.

Due to circumstances and conditions—she was the oldest at 10 and no support systems were around—she was having to serve as mother to Cipriano and me and shortly thereafter to Juan. That marked the beginning of a life of having to care for others. From there on until her death, she maintained what we jokingly refer to as an open-door policy. Anyone, family or not, from anywhere, for any reason whatsoever, could come in and stay. And many did. Many came and stayed for extended periods of time. There was always room at the inn.

One example of many is when Tio Cipriano came from Mexico very ill and stayed with her for months until she nursed him back to health, then Cundi and his cancer, and the list goes on.

Cundi's mother, Dona Catalina, for many years was not able to take care of herself. With Cundi's help, Neg refused to turn her over to assisted living and took care of her until she died.

I suppose we are all subject to have periods in our lives of crisis, pain and suffering. Neg had her share of that from early on. I believe this gave Neg an affinity to recognize it in others. Neg was a remarkable lady with a remarkable combination of strength and compassion. I believe some, at some level, would draw strength or comfort from her. That would explain how there were people always visiting her. This had to be very draining and eventually impacted her health.

I will always be grateful to Guero (my oldest son). When time took its toll and the time came when she needed to be taken care of, he surfaced. After many years of absence, he came back to Arizona. In obedience to his love for her, he decided to put his life on hold and came back to be with her and take care of her 24-7.

He came back in November 2012. He kept her company to the end, September 4, 2015. They were always joking, making fun of each other, he would take her places, drive around, etc. Whenever possible, without Neg knowing, he discouraged would-be visitors from dropping by.

In that respect, it was only fitting that she would be at the receiving end of loving care from those dear to her in the home she loved, among the plants she had nursed for a lifetime. Life owed her nothing less than that!

The visiting nurse warned us she most likely would not survive the night. There were quite a few of us. We were taking turns being with her. Figs are her favorite treat, but she's not allowed to have them because of the seeds. She asks for one, and we give it to her. Some of us are with her in her bedroom, some in the living room, some overflow on to the porch.

I go out on the porch after being with her. Cousin Lina is there. We see each other's faces and out of sadness, burst into song and impromptu serenade her:

Que linda está la mañana
En que vengo a saludarte
Venimos todos con gusto
Y placer a felicitarte
El día que tu naciste
Nacieron todas las flores
En la pila del bautismo
Cantaron los ruiseñores
Levántate de mañana
Mira que ya amaneció,

It served to express to her our love for her, and for us, by this action, loosen up clogged channels and allow for the release of the immense sadness invading us.

By virtue of the love you inspired in us, you made us all much better human beings.

Emilio Noir

EN (Emilio Noir) has been up all night. It's been cold and rainy. The chill reaches his weary bones. Dawn's first light seems like a promise, but he knows better. He's been that cold before! The one teardrop, mixed with a raindrop, roll down his cheek and make it to his lip. The sudden bittersweet taste interrupts his deep reverie. Maybe the timing is right to see what is bugging him.

Ey Emilio, what's up old friend, are you having one of those moments? I am here for you, old buddy! Silence ah? I'm not surprised. Come on, complain about something. This is your chance! (More silence.) Damn it, Emilio, you are one weird guy! What are you moping about?

May I remind you that just recently you were being rushed in a gurney through the corridors of a hospital with shouts of "Heart attack! Heart attack!" Some odd ball you are! One would expect that at a moment like that your entire life history would be parading before you. Or you would be in some kind of panic at the prospect of the consequences of what was taking place. Instead, you were thinking how impressed you were by the professionalism and level of efficiency shown by those around you at those moments! The surgery room felt like a meat locker: the stainless-steel table is hard and cold, like a block of ice. As the nurses are stripping you naked, you don't have an ounce of self-decorum! You remind me of Kramer at the Calvin Klein office posing in his underwear.

Speaking of which, you are pissing me off with your silence. How can you lay in that block of ice, occupied with being thankful and grateful to all of those around you, being grateful to whatever in their life brought them to that moment in time, thankful for what they represent, whatever the outcome might be? You are the one that has been critical of the health professional industry infrastructure your entire life. You claim that those who write the prescriptions, those who do the surgeries, etc. don't have the balls to, in spite of all their pseudo, higher-than-thou education, change the system. You claim it would be for their own good to not be under the thumb of those above them, the thumb that pushes them toward a lifestyle full of false values. Never mind, you don't have to answer any of that. I apologize, that is not even the subject we want to cover here.

Still silent ah? You are such a pain in the ass. You remain fascinated by boring things. You were enchanted when you found out that you can change water into ice, steam, etc., but you can't destroy it. You were blown away by the fact that people still believe that you can pass time by killing time. You can't kill time; time kills you. And yet, time can't kill consciousness. So what if thought is flawed?

You piss me off, Emilio! You are forever looking for knowledge but struggle to remember that knowledge is not everything, just like you forget that having all the facts or all the experience is not enough. I do give you credit, though, that in those moments, when facing overwhelming grief, you managed to learn that you can only cure grief with laughter.

You bastard, you have heard the siren song many times. She promises you the song is a wedding song. But first, she says a toast, and you know that the intoxicating drink she offers you is a mix of your own tears and your own blood! And you drink, and yet again, you walk up to the altar. You are impressed by her wedding dress. Upon seeing her necklace, you think, *What a beautiful pearl necklace!* You idiot, those are not pearls, they are your tears. And you know she will deny herself in marriage! Tell me, Emilio, what kind of game is this? Can I play it? (EN finally breaks his silence.) Sure, you can play it, *if you have the balls!*

EN. What are you complaining about any way, you pussy!
Me. You wanna know? You wanna know? You are a thorn on my side.
I have to put up with you! You are enamored with the April of the poets. Amid the melee of sounds in the world, you discern the song! And the song puts an energy in your chest, and you feel on top of the world. You want to walk into the court and play yet another game. And every time you take me in there with you, we both end up going down. Every time you say, "Next time is going to be different." You parasite!
EN. Fuck you, chuy! You know you can't live without me! You count on me to tell you what you want to hear. You are as eager as I

am to keep playing this game. It suits you fine that it is a four-wall court game. You hit the hard ball with your bare hands. Depending on the way you hit it, that's the way it's coming back. Even though it's a doubles game and there are four players on the court, the ball is always coming at you. The location of this court is in this third dimensional, relative world. You play by the rules dictated by time and space. The one rule that everyone best knows but chooses to ignore is that you don't break the rules; they break you. The four players are you, me, Life and its doubles partner and side kick, Thought. It is my duty, and I exist to tell you what you want to hear. So here it goes:

At the tender age when you, the Sonoran Collective, were challenged, your challenger, Life, thought you guys were going to be easy pickings. And yet, with the odds against you, you never asked for clemency. Setback after setback, Neg got us all to a mindset where we can see our world as one where we live in harmony with our surroundings; may they be organic or otherwise. Today, since you represent the Sonoran Collective, I hereby, by the power vested in me by you, I officially declare you, the Sonoran Collective, a winner in this game. This is not because at 82 you hold a full-time construction job, not because you are where you want to be, doing what you want to do, not because you have everything—if you don't have it, you don't need it—not because in this relative world you have excellent health.

I declare you victorious because after all these years, the ups and downs, you and life remain in excellent terms. You are triumphant because in the middle of this constant bombardment, you can still hear the song. In other words, my friend, you win because you are one blessed, happy, lucky bastard. Speaking of which, hey, do you hear that? It must be April again! What do you say, chuy, do you wanna?

ME. I do hear! And do wanna! What te hey! Here are my balls! Let's go play!

Please note that as they walk toward the court, arm in arm, they know that *this is the beginning of a beautiful friendship.*

Emilio Noir about to step into the court, to play yet another game

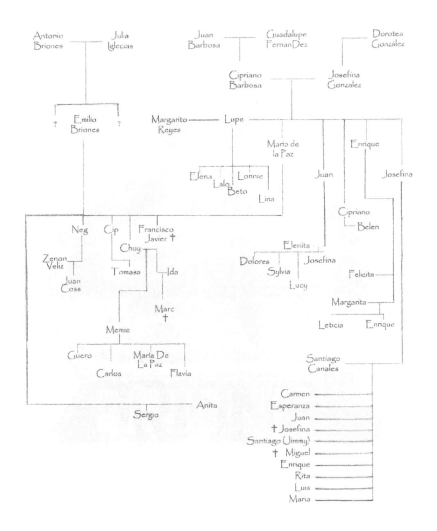

Printed in the USA
CPSIA information can be obtained
at www.ICGtesting.com
LVHW022256290524
781384LV00011B/454